DATE DUE

NOV.27. 1991	SEP.15.1998		
FEB.01.1992	FEB.12.1999		
APR.21.1992			
JUL.22.1992	APR.14.1999		
FEB.02.1993	APR.27.2000		
JUN.15.1993	JA 25 '01		
AUG.06.1993	MAR 2 2 2001		
NOV.03.1993	NOV 1 7 2001		
SEP.06.1994			
NOV.19.1994			
MAR09.1995			
JUL.18.1995			
JAN.03.1996			
NOV.16.1995			
MAR12.1997			
JAN.29.1998			

HIGHSMITH   #LO-45220

ONE
ON
ONE

ONE
ON
ONE

Win the Interview,
Win the Job

THEODORE T. PETTUS

Random House · New York

Library of Congress Cataloging in Publication Data
Pettus, Theodore.
One on one.
1. Employment interviewing. 2. Applications for positions. I. Title.
HF5549.5.I6P47   650.1′4   81–40211
ISBN 0–394–52138–2   AACR2

Manufactured in the United States of America
468975

TO:
Peggy, Thorpe, Scotty, Thomas and Fran,
. . . all very successful one-on-one people

Contents

ONE
ON
ONE

Five Things You Must Do Before You Dare Have an Interview

Don't read any more books about getting a job

Understand the job market

Know the company

Do an FBI number on the interviewer

Lay back until you're ready

Tʜɪs book will show you how to get a job. Not just any job, but the job you really want. It will succeed if you know what you want to do and if you have some idea of whom you want to work for.

The proven and carefully researched technique that I will describe can work for anybody who is willing to take it seriously. It makes no difference how old you are, what sex you are, your level of education, your job history, or even the kind of job you are after.

Recent graduates looking for their first job will discover how to virtually eliminate their competition and save themselves months of misdirected energy.

Currently employed individuals trapped in low-paying, dead-end jobs will discover how to maximize their earning and career potential by quickly obtaining the exciting job offers they deserve.

People between jobs will learn how immediately to sidestep the anxiety and frustration they are now experiencing by discovering just how easy it is to land new jobs which offer more remuneration and challenge than anything they have held previously.

This book will not help you discover yourself or restructure your life. That exercise is in the hands of the clergy, pop psychologists and headshrinkers. Nor will it help you pick your profession. Carpenters who want to be corporate executives, professors who want to start earning big money in private business will not find any secrets in these pages. But if you are the kind of person who already knows what you are after, this book will make sure that you get it.

My thesis is simple. *Nobody has ever gotten a job offer of any kind, at any salary, at any point in history without first having that one-on-one meeting known as the interview.*

For too long, misdirected job applicants and advice-peddling professionals have treated this crucial thirty-minute meeting as though it hardly matters. In fact, the interview is *all* that matters. Win the interview and you'll get hired!

Most job seekers today fail to get the jobs they really want because something went wrong in an interview they were not prepared to take. In this book you will learn how to create a thirty-minute miracle. How to set up an interview, how to prepare for it correctly, and how to conduct yourself properly . . . one on one. In short, how to get hired.

DON'T READ ANY MORE BOOKS ABOUT GETTING A JOB

At last count, I discovered more than seventy books on this painful subject. Read them all and you'll surely be employed as a lifetime patient in some mental hospital. Read just a few of them and you'll find yourself getting more confused than you are right now. While many contain some very good advice, they dispense a great deal of superfluous and sometimes contradictory methodology. But worst of all, virtually every current title slights your biggest single concern, the interview.

If there is one thing that all successful people have in common, it is their ability to use their time efficiently. "Time is everything," lectures Joyce C. Hall, chairman of Hallmark Cards, Inc. "Anything you want, anything you accomplish—pleasure, success, fortune—is measured in time." As a person who has yet to be offered the job of your dreams, your time is pure gold. And every day you waste is costing you innumerable lost opportunities and, ultimately, money.

By necessity, looking for a job must be a full-time occupation if you are going to be truly successful. This means that if you are currently employed, you must be prepared to make sacrifices. For a short period all of your leisure time and even some of your time on the job must be focused on your job hunt. If you are just out of school or currently unemployed, plan on spending 10 hours a day on this important project. *It is infinitely more difficult to land a great job than it is to keep one.* Begin now to prepare yourself for a short burst of incredibly intense energy and discipline which will produce some remarkable job offers.

But you need a job now, this very second, right? Wrong. You need the best job you can get. You need the highest salary you can possibly earn. You need a job that won't turn to drudgery after six months. You need an employer who will recognize your talents and will promote you rapidly. You need to work with people you respect and who appreciate you. You need to wake up every morning just itching to get to work and come home at night still brimming with excitement.

If you are willing to settle for less, you are making your first serious mistake. Henry J. Kaiser, one of America's greatest industrialists, cautioned, "Many people have grand dreams. But they feel these dreams are impossible. They shilly-shally around, wasting their time on routine jobs. If you think you don't know what you want to do, just ask yourself, 'What do I want most out of life?' That's your dream. And no matter how silly and farfetched it appears, you can achieve it." But prepare to work hard.

UNDERSTAND THE JOB MARKET

Back in the early seventies, in the middle of a serious economic recession, oil billionaire John Paul Getty boldly announced: "In over fifty years as an active businessman, I've never seen anything to equal the current prevailing climate of opportunity." In light of record unemployment figures and faltering production, most people thought the oil billionaire had lost his mind. But he was absolutely correct. In fact, today his optimism sounds understated.

The rest of the world has always been amazed by the mobility of America's population. First from the farms to the cities. Then from the small cities to the large ones. Then coast to coast, south to north, north to south, and so on.

But the really amazing statistics are not geographical. Americans change jobs and careers to a degree unparalleled in history. The typical American worker over thirty-five years of age changes jobs once every three years. The average working man or woman under thirty-five is out looking for a new job every year and a half! Are the bulk of these job switchers locked into unrewarding, low-paying manual trades? Not at all. *Psychology Today* reports: "Laborers find their jobs more satisfying than anyone else —more than managers, more than clerks, more than salesmen. And professional or technical workers enjoy their jobs less than anyone else."

A recent study on "Work in America" by Columbia University revealed that the overwhelming majority of Americans, 90 percent, would prefer an occupation other than their present one.

In most countries, and until recently in America, too, people rarely change jobs and almost never switch careers. But those days are over. And this is nothing but good news for you because every person who leaves one job for another has created an opportunity for you. Every day countless thousands of high-paying jobs with good companies are opening up. Many of these are high-quality openings that will continue to develop regardless of the state of the economy. These are wonderful opportunities that you will soon be taking advantage of.

For some strange reason, however, most job seekers fail to recognize this situation, preferring the company of gloom-and-doom prophets. Wallowing in self-pity, most job seekers seem to enjoy pointing at unemployment statistics as some kind of excuse for accepting jobs far below the ideal they once dreamed of. At the same time, miserably employed men and women cling tenaciously to boring, dead-end jobs, too frightened to come to terms with some mythical breadline. Those who have been recently fired prop this statistical crutch under their arm as they cast about for sympathy and understanding.

Unemployment figures have virtually no effect on your ability to find the job you want. Paine Webber, Inc., the

prestigious Wall Street investment firm, recently decided
to analyze 7-percent-unemployment figures. Here's what
they found:

- 1% were looking for work for the first time.
- 2% were re-entering the job market, having voluntarily
  withdrawn.
- 1% quit their jobs.
- 1% were laid off temporarily.
- 2% were fired.

In other words, "less than half the unemployed had
been laid off, and a third of these were simply waiting to
be recalled. The rest would find jobs in six or seven
weeks."

KNOW THE COMPANY

The majority of job applicants who fail to get hired all
make the same mistake. They don't know the company
they are interviewing. Even the most inept interviewer
can sniff out this ignorance in a matter of seconds and
from then on the candidate is hopelessly on the defensive,
having revealed that he didn't care enough about the job
to bother investigating the company.

Donald M. Kendall, chairman of PepsiCo, makes no
bones about it. "I'm turned off at a first meeting by people
who haven't done their homework." In her book, *How to
Talk to Practically Anybody about Practically Anything,* Barbara
Walters cites her own experience. "It is almost impossible
to maintain poise when you are scared to death," says
Walters. "My best advice for dealing with destructive
anxiety is *homework* . . . homework helps enormously when
you apply for a job."

If you are a student or recent graduate, investigate the company you want to work for as though you were going to write a 200-page thesis on it. If you already have a job, try to learn as much about your employer-to-be as you already know about your present employer.

Begin by finding out exactly what the company does or makes. Never make the kind of mistake a college classmate of mine did while being interviewed by IC Industries (formerly Illinois Central Railroad). Halfway through his interview, while things were going well, my friend announced that all his life he had wanted to be in the railroad business. The man across the desk blanched and quickly terminated the discussion. Why? The job in question had absolutely nothing whatsoever to do with the railroads.

There is no better place than your local library to begin your research. Enlist the help of a librarian to investigate the company in some, if not all, of the following sources.

Chamber of Commerce publications
Dun & Bradstreet's Million Dollar Directory
Encyclopedia of Business Information
Fitch Corporation Manuals
F and S Indexes
Fortune 500 Issue
MacRae's Blue Book
Moody's Industrial Manual
National Trade and Professional Assoc. Pubs.
Plan Purchasing Directory
Poor's Register of Corporations, Directory & Executives
Standard and Poor's Corporation Records, Industrial
    Index, and Listed Stock Reports
Statistical Abstract of the U.S. (Dept. Comm.)
Thomas' Register of American Manufacturers
Walkers Manual of Far Western Corporations
    & Securities

Be sure to take copious notes, paying particular attention to the names of major officers, new developments in the company, etc.

At the same time, tap the company directly or through friends for as much reading material as you can find. Ask for recruitment brochures, company publications of all kinds, even detailed information on various products or services the company may offer.

In the case of publicly held companies, those who have stock held by outsiders, it is vitally important that you get a current copy of their annual report. This document, above all others, is required reading. If you have trouble understanding it, find someone who can explain it to you. Get a clear picture of where this company is going: what its current financial status is, its record of growth, its position in the industry.

Begin to read the business press to keep abreast of current developments. If you are interested in a large company, the *Wall Street Journal, Barron's, Forbes* and *Business Week* are compulsory reading. All businesses have their own trade magazines and newsletters. Find out which ones are important and start reading them. Look for all news that might affect hiring decisions: new contracts, accounts, successful new-product introductions, lawsuits, etc.

Starting today, make a serious effort to contact someone who works for the company. Through friends, relatives, friends of friends, arrange to meet one or two people who can give you firsthand, inside information.

Make a list of all the company's major officers. Look them up in a *Who's Who.* Find out what kind of people makes it into this company's senior management. Do they have similar backgrounds, education, training? To understand what any organization is about, it is essential to have a clear picture of their leaders. F. Perry Wilson, former chairman of Union Carbide, advised young job seekers, "In the last analysis, it is the management and, particularly, the chief executive officer who sets the moral and ethical tone for a corporation."

If you listen to what members of top management say in speeches and in the press, what they do in practice, you will have no trouble deciding whether this company is the one for you. And just as important, you will know how to approach them for an interview.

For example, Donald N. Frey, chairman of Bell & Howell Company, revealed to *Business Week* his attitude about hiring employees from outside the company. "We needed new thoughts on a financial function that had become inbred," Frey admitted. "Inbreeding causes you to talk among yourselves. And when this happens the world may move beyond you." Not only is Frey's attitude about hiring outsiders unusual among large industrial corporations, it offers strong encouragement to someone seriously interested in working for Bell & Howell.

Someone interested in retailing might have discovered the same thing by reading about Joseph Brooks, chairman of Lord & Taylor, in *Chain Store Age* magazine. "I think it is terribly important for every company in this day and age to bring in outsiders. As the business expands it's a healthy thing in the executive capacity to have 10% new blood brought in every year."

On the other hand, anyone who seriously listened to the management of Exxon, Kodak, ITT and dozens of other large corporations would quickly discover that outsiders stand a much smaller chance of slipping into corporate management. These companies like to promote from within.

Some companies are quite candid in revealing their needs and problems. A job candidate interested in Xerox could have gathered key information simply by reading the company newspaper. In one issue, Xerox's president David Kearns stated that "our first-line management is not communicating clearly and does not represent a real force in giving information and a feeling of confidence to our people."

Experts tell us that major corporate officers, from the chairman on down, devote as much as 24% of their time looking for new personnel inside and outside their companies. Knowing what these top men think, remembering what they have said and putting these data to use in your interview can be very effective, if not decisive, in landing hard-to-get jobs.

An applicant being interviewed by even the lowest-level company employee can immediately gain an upper hand the second he demonstrates a clear knowledge of what his interviewer's boss thinks about something.

Several years ago a senior at Radcliffe College threw the fear of God into her startled interviewer at Citibank when she began quoting Walter Wriston, the bank's chairman. Sensing the interview was not going well at all, she began rattling off Mr. Wriston's public statements on the importance of placing more women in the bank's national division. The young interviewer immediately rushed her down the hall for a second interview. She was offered a job the following week. Needless to say, if this woman had been lucky enough to be interviewed by Mr. Wriston himself, she might have been able to significantly improve her starting salary!

The interviewing process is a very expensive proposition for any company. A large corporation must maintain a well-staffed personnel department, which makes no direct contribution to the product or service that the company provides. When company management does the actual interviewing, the costs in time and productivity are even greater. A typical diversified manufacturing company spends more than $20,000 recruiting each person for managerial or professional positions.

For this reason it is not hard to understand why interviews are hard to get and why it is imperative that you do your homework and know the company you're talking to.

DO AN FBI NUMBER ON THE INTERVIEWER

After you have learned everything you can about the company, after you have memorized the names of the major officers, after you've read enough, heard enough, absorbed enough information to deliver an extended speech—then you're ready for the next crucial step. It's time to find out who the lucky person is who gets to interview you.

If you are interested in a small company, that is relatively easy. For a large company this job can be infuriatingly difficult. Regardless, this is no time for short cuts. You are about to do another vital piece of research which your competition in the marketplace has totally ignored. You are building a competitive advantage which, if used correctly, will be devastatingly effective.

All of us, whether we choose to admit it or not, are naturally suspicious of the unfamiliaar. Blind faith in other people went out the window in our early childhood. President Reagan feels infinitely more comfortable in the White House surrounded with men he has known in the past and who share his conservative philosophy. Nobody questions that there are probably thousands of more talented aides he could tap for service, but could he trust them? Would they demonstrate the kind of loyalty he demands? Could he go to sleep at night confident that crucial government business was in safe hands?

Business people are no different. A strong résumé packed with wonderful credentials is no guarantee to a nervous company treasurer that a prospective accountant won't take off for Costa Rica with company money. A distinguished-looking applicant with an impressive list of references can still destroy a company by leaking manufacturing secrets to the competition.

Companies, both large and small, are like families. They can tolerate an incredible amount of infighting, but woe be to the outsider who questions their intentions! Successful businesses demand loyalty from their people. And they usually get it. Even the largest multinational corporation has an instinctive suspicion of new faces. "Loyalty is the greatest characteristic trait needed in an executive," Charles P. McCormick (McCormick Spice Co.) once confided to John Paul Getty. James E. Robinson, chairman of Indian Head Mills, ranked loyalty ahead of the ability to lead.

Loyalty can't be built overnight. But if in your first encounter you can give your interviewer one reason why he should trust you any more than the next guy off the street, you have a gigantic advantage. And one sure way to gain that advantage is to *know the person across the desk.*

Begin by finding out the interviewer's name and title. Remember, you are initiating the meeting, and in many cases, you have control over who will interview you. If you are after a sales position in a medium-sized company, start with the vice president in charge of sales. Find out if he does his own interviewing, and if not, then who does? Be careful to pick someone with real power over the hiring situation. Avoid executives on the eve of retirement. They're probably losing interest in their jobs, and their company is already looking beyond them.

In very small companies you should focus on the top one or two people. The chances are not likely that they would let the responsibility for hiring slip from their control.

Large companies present a problem. The name of that problem is the personnel department. You must determine what role the personnel department plays in the hiring process. Traditionally, personnel people have represented the very bottom of the interviewing ladder. Recently, however, this situation has been changing. Some corporations have integrated their major personnel executives into the management of the company. Some, but not many; for the most part, Personnel continues to be a collection of virtually powerless individuals whose major function is to protect management's precious time by screening out undesirable candidates.

If you are interested in a job with a large company, you must decide whether to go through Personnel or try an end run directly to the person who does the hiring. Companies have strict policies on this matter, and with some investigation you should be able to find out what the policy is. In either case, remember one thing: while the personnel people may be the butt of intercompany gossip, they can destroy your chances of being hired. Therefore, tread lightly. Be careful that their noses don't get out of joint if you do an end run. Don't be condescending if you are forced to begin your interviewing in their department.

After you have established the interviewer's name and title (it might be a good idea to research two or three interviewers), begin digging into his background. Find out how long he has been with the company. If it has been a short time, who was his previous employer? His previous title? Find out where he went to school, where he grew up, what his outside interests are, where he lives. If you know other people in the company, quiz them in detail about your interviewer's personality, reputation, role in the company. What kind of people has he hired in the past? Dig for information until you know as much about him as you would about a relative you never met but have heard about all your life. Pretend you are J. Edgar Hoover.

What is the purpose of all of this? The purpose is to give you an interviewing advantage simply not available to the other two hundred people he has interviewed in the last twelve months. Because when it finally comes time for you to sit down in his office, you'll know more about him than he knows about you, even if your résumé is ten pages long! And because you know him, you'll be in an excellent position to guide the interview toward your strong points, away from your weak points.

The former chairman of the board of an international advertising agency was dumfounded when a student asked him how things were going with the Canadian National Opera. "How did you know I was a director?" asked the chairman. "I read it in *Who's Who,*" the young man replied. Guess who got hired?

One word of caution. Just because you have amassed a great deal of information about your interviewer doesn't mean you have to use it all. Exercise common sense and subtlety. You must not give him the impression that you have been snooping behind his back. Don't try to force the conversation toward non-job-related topics. Don't pretend you are someone or something you are not. Be yourself.

LAY BACK UNTIL YOU'RE READY

The temptation can be irresistible. You know the company you want to work for. You know the name of the man who does the interviewing and hiring. And you know they need someone with your skills right now. So why not give him a call? Or send in your résumé? STOP! Unless you have done *all* your homework on the company, unless you have seriously investigated the man who will soon be investigating you, unless you are physically and psychologically ready . . . you may destroy your chances of getting the job you want. John Paul Getty warned young job seekers, "Before a beginner can begin, his biggest job is that of appraising—not praising—himself."

Let me repeat the most important lesson in this book. *Most people fail to get the job they really want. The reason they fail is not that they are not qualified. They fail because something went wrong in an interview which they were not prepared for.*

Under intense questioning most candidates reveal a basic ignorance about some fundamental aspect of the company's business. Zappo! They're in big trouble. Even worse, because they are nervous they disclose negative, unasked-for information about themselves. Double zappo! And on top of all of this, because they have failed to investigate the interviewer, they are held at the mercy of *his* line of questioning and are not prepared to control the interview to their own advantage.

One of the most destructive aspects of being interviewed before you are ready is psychological. If in your heart you know that you are not completely prepared, ready to answer any question, eager to ask some of your own . . . your body will flash the message to your interviewer before your tongue finishes you off. In such a situation, not one person in a thousand can fake confidence. Your posture gives you away as you hunch up your shoulders or wring your hands. Your eyes avoid his as you desperately dodge a difficult question about your past. Your voice loses its evenness. Once you feel that you are in trouble you become increasingly tense, you lose your sense of humor, and most important, you lose your self-respect.

The business community is a very small world. By the time you isolate the kind of business you want to be in and the specific job you want, you are talking about a small number of available job openings with only a handful of companies. When you walk in unprepared and have a negative interview, not only have you lost the job you came for, you have lost much more. You have lost a crack at other openings in the same company. You have lost the ability to ask your interviewer if he knows of any other openings at competitive companies. You've even lost the chance to receive helpful criticism on your interviewing style.

No matter how anxious you are to get your first job or get off the unemployment line or get out of the job you now have . . . lay back until you are ready, really ready, to have that interview.

TWO

How to Meet the Person Who Is Going to Hire You

Don't be afraid to use people

A letter he can't ignore

Help Wanted ads—a different perspective

Beware of the telephone

Headhunters, body snatchers, campus
interviewers and meat racks

I T is actually possible, in fact alarmingly common, for people to have hundreds of interviews during their working career and still never get the job they really wanted. Most people begin and end their working years willing, even anxious to compromise their goals with what they assume to be the harsh realities of the marketplace. Often this is an attitude developed during childhood. Sometimes it is the result of an unpleasant interview during their twenties. Parental pressure, financial strain or lack of patience can all contribute to this unnecessary tragedy. But it is never too early or too late to correct this situation and to find yourself the job that you desperately want and deserve.

Most people I know fail to get the job they want because they never sat down and talked with the person who could hire them. If this sounds too simplistic, think for a minute. Anybody, if he or she is persistent, can get an interview. Write a letter, make a phone call, drop off a résumé, and many companies, especially large companies, will have "one of our people" talk with you. But this is *not* an interview, this is a corporate obligation—an exercise in business etiquette—and usually a complete waste of time.

Students or recent graduates love to brag to one another that they had five or six interviews in one day. But what can this possibly prove if there were no job openings in the first place? Or if the interviewer is powerless to make a hiring decision?

A true interview, the only kind that matters, is one person with a job to offer talking with another person who wants that job. This chapter will tell you how to get into the same room with that person, or at the very least, get to meet the person who does his screening.

DON'T BE AFRAID TO USE PEOPLE

People who refuse to use other people have one thing in common: *failure*. The old adage that says "You gotta know someone" or "You've got to have contacts" is absolutely true despite what you may have heard to the contrary.

Henry J. Kaiser, the man who built Hoover Dam, thousands of Liberty ships, and a gigantic aluminum company, not to mention an incredible personal fortune, calmly reminded us, "You seldom accomplish very much by yourself. You must get the assistance of others." And the fact is, you do know people who can help you get the job you really want. Whether you decide to use them and use them properly is up to you.

Your most immediate and dedicated source of help are members of your family: your parents, brothers, sisters, uncles, cousins, etc. These people know you intimately. They trust you. They like you. And most important, your success or failure reflects directly on them. The famous Washington columnist and author Stewart Alsop admitted freely: "The best way to become a columnist is to have a brother who is one already." His elder brother was, of course, Joseph Alsop, the colorful, internationally syndicated columnist.

At the same time that you begin to use your family, put the word out to everyone else that you can think of. You will be surprised to discover just how many influential people you can reach.

Approach all your friends, selected classmates from grade school, high school and college. Get out your old yearbooks and alumni directories and comb through them for people you suspect may know something about the company that interests you. Focus on friends who have been particularly successful in their fields. Sift through old desk calendars and diaries. Rack your memory for the names of key people you have met in the last five years. Teachers and professors, lawyers, brokers, real estate agents, tax accountants, old bosses, newspaper and television people, priests, rabbis, insurance agents, politicians. You should have little trouble assembling an impressive list of twenty or more individuals who not only can but will be delighted to help.

Remember to take advantage of the new people you meet every day: the barber who cuts your hair . . . the man you sat next to on the airplane . . . the car dealer you were dickering with last week. Aristotle Onassis landed his first job by striking up a conversation with some fellow Greeks he happened to meet on a bus in Argentina. A senior vice president I know at a major oil company got his foot in the door by using the name of one of the building's cleaning ladies. A former lifeguard on Long Island, now a powerful airline executive, met an elderly man on the beach he found helpful. The man turned out to be Juan Trippe, the retired chairman of Pan Am!

How you use these people is crucially important. Just as you should never set up an interview before you have done all your homework, *you must not approach others for help until you know exactly what you are after.* Once you have a clear idea of what you want to do and of the companies you would consider working for, and have developed a solid understanding of what these companies are all about, you are ready.

If the people you use are going to take you seriously, you must let them share in the adventure you are undertaking. They must have a sense of the confidence that you have in yourself. This means putting your ego in the back seat. Everyone knows jobs are difficult to get. And nobody is going to make fun of you or hold anything against you if you fail to land a particular position. On the other hand, when you do get that job offer, just watch them gather around taking full credit for your success!

While family members are more tolerant of your behavior, don't take advantage of it. Don't disappoint them by going off half-cocked. They will forgive you, but their friends and contacts won't.

If the person you are using offers to call or write someone at a company that interests you, by all means encourage him to do so. Make sure that you give him a copy of your résumé as well as a short verbal description of who you are and what you are after. Let him share in your enthusiasm and dedication for the job you want. Make sure he knows how much you appreciate his help.

If he doesn't offer to contact the company in your behalf, don't hesitate to ask him to. Does he know anyone who might know someone? Does he know any ex-employees? Ask him, politely, to keep his ears open. And give him your phone number, in case he runs across something. If you feel he is an especially valuable person, don't hesitate to call him at a later date, reminding him who you are and what you are after.

Harold Geneen, the genius who turned ITT around by acquiring 250 different companies, like Avis, Hartford Insurance and Continental Baking, says, "I believe that you don't have to go looking for a valuable man—he reveals himself automatically." And how does this happen "automatically"? Most of the time someone whispers in his ear, drops a name, makes a suggestion.

Always make it your policy to keep track of all the people you are using—their full name, title, business adress. Always ask them before you use their name, being careful to give them a clear idea of *how* you will use it. When they mention the names of employees at the company you want to work for, take detailed notes. Find out about that particular person's title and responsibility. Dig for details of the relationship between the two people.

Using people to "get in the door" is perfectly acceptable behavior. In many businesses it is the only way people get hired. Texas Congresswoman Barbara Jordan makes no secret of her abilities in this area. "I sought the power points. I knew that if I were to get anything done, they would be the ones to help me get it done."

However, this never means you should take advantage of someone's good will, exploit a friend or lie. Be extremely careful that you do not misrepresent the extent of the friendship between you and the person you are using. Don't misquote him or say anything that would put him in an embarrassing position. And it goes without saying, do not use anybody who might introduce negative elements.

Finally, be sure to *thank* the persons who have helped you. And do it *in writing.* In your letter tell them specifically why they were helpful. That important letter will plant your name firmly in their memory and encourage them to help you again in the future.

A LETTER HE CAN'T IGNORE

The overwhelming percentage of all interviews are initiated by a letter from the applicant to the interviewer/company. People in the personnel field call this a "broadcast letter." Traditionally, it is a short, to-the-point request to be considered for employment attached to an applicant's résumé.

It has been estimated that in a recent one-year period America's employers received more than 25 million letters with résumés. A large employer like AT&T received an estimated 600,000 letters in 1977 and hired fewer than 100,000 new people.

It may come as sad news, but *your résumé will not get you hired. Your qualifications will not get you hired. You will only get hired when you win the interview.* And you can't win one until you get one.

Dozens of candid employers I've talked with admit that *most résumés never get read*! Most are routed directly to the typing pool, where an indifferent secretary pecks out a customized form letter telling you that XYZ Company "has no openings at this time." An increasing number of profit-squeezed companies don't even honor you with a reply letter.

The only hearing the majority of job applicants ever get is the ten seconds it takes some lower-level executive to read your cover letter. *Ten seconds!* Needless to say, your letter better be good! Fortunately, you have a terrific advantage. Most cover letters, easily 90 percent, are absolute disasters. They are trite, colorless, vapid and numbingly dull.

Your ability to write powerful letters is an essential business skill. General Tire & Rubber's L. A. McQueen offers an opinion few employers would argue with. "People judge you by what you say and write. I don't know a successful man in business who is not a good letter writer." One badly composed letter to a company you really care about is an unforgivable sin. It destroys a precious opportunity you may never have again.

The most common mistake among job-seeking letter writers appears right on the front of the envelope. It is addressed to the wrong person! Or even worse, it is simply addressed to the company or the personnel department. If you have done your homework (detailed in Chapter 1), you will know who does the hiring and therefore to whom to write. Until you know that person's name, title and something about him . . . put your stationery away.

Many employment counselors and others have convinced applicants that employers need you more than you need them. This may be true after your interview, but not before. Until they meet you face to face, listen to you talk, ask you some tough questions, you are just another stranger. And people coming off the street demanding fat salaries or expensive training programs are something they have plenty of.

Operating under a tidal wave of applications, most employers develop a nasty cynicism toward job hunters. You may find it comforting to believe that your letters and résumés are received with eagerness and anticipation. You may conjure up a picture of some distinguished executive in his wood-paneled office who has suddenly discovered that his problems are over because your letter has arrived. But unless you are applying to the U.S. Army, you are way off base.

It may seem cruel to say so, but when you begin to compose your letter, assume that the people who will receive it don't like you. Assume that they find your talents worthless. Assume that there is only a small chance that they will be willing to embarrass themselves in front of their bosses by suggesting that perhaps you should be interviewed.

If you assume all of this, then you won't join the one million applicants this month who will begin their letters with "I understand you have an opening for . . ." or "I am looking for a job as . . ." Instead, you will push your typewriter back, get out a pencil and spend a couple of hours deciding just how you are going to convince a deeply cynical person why you are any better than the thirty other applicants whose letters he has just rejected.

"Your writing style is as unique as your thumbprint," says William Brady, Jr., former director of alumni placement at Northeastern University. "No one can draft a letter or write your résumé for you." And I'm certainly not going to try. I also suggest that you be careful taking anybody else's advice. What I will suggest, however, is a framework that has proved successful.

The letter that produces an interview—and this is all you can expect from your letter—should contain the following elements:

1. It must *introduce* you.
2. It must *tease* the reader's interest by presenting interesting information about you.
3. It must present a *clear knowledge* of his business.
4. It must appear to *offer more to the reader* than to the writer.
5. It must have a style that shows you know *how to write.*
6. It must be *original,* without being freaky.

Because you have done your homework and know the person you are writing to, use what you have learned. Like most people, your interviewer is more interested in himself than he is in you. So approach him on familiar ground. If you can locate an article he has written or a speech he has delivered, use this material to your advantage. "I just read your article on international management and I was curious to know how you felt about . . ." Right away you have flattered him by your interest. And at the same time you have demonstrated that the two of you have something in common. Further, by asking intelligent questions you have obligated him to reply. Suddenly, your letter has been separated from the others he received that morning.

Sometimes articles and speeches are hard to find or simply don't exist. Then you may wish to approach him with a question, observation or suggestion that pertains directly to his field. Once again, be certain that you have done your homework. You can't afford to appear naive or transparent.

"Someone has *got* to give ideas to industry," remarks a cynical new product manager. "You'd be amazed how slow we are at thinking them up for ourselves." If you have had sales experience, for example, you may want to make a suggestion in an area where he is clearly weak. "While observing one of your salesmen calling on

the B & J Hardware Company, I couldn't help noticing
that . . ." For students or others who have little work
experience, the power of keen observation can be most
effective. "Recently, while purchasing a can of your tile
cleaner, I noticed that Safeway had placed your product
in the section with detergents. Have you considered that
sales might improve if your cleaner was located with
bathroom products?"

Again referring back to your homework, you may find
that it is effective to use the name of a person who is a
mutual acquaintance. But simply dropping a recognized
name is not enough. You must firmly connect that name
with your qualifications; the days of hiring old school
chums are long gone. For example: "Ben Johnson suggested that I write you because he felt you might be
interested in some of my ideas on food processing." Here
you are offering an employer a recognized skill that comes
fully endorsed by his Saturday-morning golf partner.
This ploy may work, and it may flop. But you can be
guaranteed of getting more attention than most other applicants.

If you choose not to have somebody endorse you, it
may suffice to use him merely as a source of reliable
information: "I heard Mr. Fred Childs mention that your
research department was seriously understaffed and I
wanted to suggest . . ."

You may want to use the name of someone you have
never even met: "I recently read in *Automotive News* that
your chairman, Mr. Wilson, was exploring the possibility
of expanding distribution into Virginia. As a recent graduate of the University of Virginia, perhaps I . . ."

Whatever approach you take in your letter, you must

offer the reader something. You must seduce him into scanning your résumé. You must spark his curiosity. You must say something about you, him, his company or his company's product that makes your interview absolutely inevitable.

Your language must be clear, refreshing and very easy to read. Spelling, grammar, continuity of thought are incredibly important. Reflecting on a General Electric study, retired GE senior vice president Hershner Cross remarked, "Almost *all* graduates need improvement in their communications ability, in writing and speaking the King's English." If you are just out of school, remember that most companies are interested in your development potential, not what miracles you will perform during your first couple of years. "This communications deficiency," continues Cross, "becomes more critical later on, of course, when we have to evaluate those who want to pursue careers in management."

Just as you wouldn't show up for an interview wearing shorts and a T-shirt, take care how you present yourself in your letter. If you haven't already, invest in some decent stationery, standard 8 1/2" × 11" business stationery with your name and address printed conservatively at the top. Northeastern University's William Brady, Jr., suggests, "Select quality 'rag bond' stationery with matching envelopes. Have your résumé printed on the same stock. And use a quality electric typewriter for actual typing."

Do not use your company's business stationery if you are currently employed. This is the quickest way to have your present employer find out what you are up to. And be certain to keep a carbon copy of all letters you send.

You'll need them for reference when the time comes to show up for your interview.

HELP WANTED ADS—A DIFFERENT PERSPECTIVE

Using newspaper and magazine classified ads is the laziest possible way to look for a job. This fact, no doubt, explains their incredible popularity. Use them as your only source of opportunities and you cripple your chances of success. Use them as most job hunters do and you will destroy more opportunities than you'll discover.

By their very nature, Help Wanted ads force you into direct competition with the largest number of candidates for only a tiny fraction of America's job openings. The overwhelming percentage of jobs, perhaps 85 percent, are never advertised at all. The company fills these openings from within by hiring friends of current employees, by putting the word out among the competitive community, by using executive search firms who call people they know, or by tapping some lucky applicant who just happened to write a timely letter.

Make no mistake about it. Any ad you read was preceded by a massive internal and external manhunt that failed miserably. The ad you read in today's paper is appealing to the court of last resort—the general public. It represents a frantic S O S that was placed at great reluctance by the company in need.

Why do companies hate to advertise job openings? For one thing, they are expensive. A tiny 2" announcement in the Los Angeles *Times* costs $90. An ad the size of a cigarette pack in the *Wall Street Journal* costs $300. A series of newspaper ads running on a daily basis might cost a company $8,000 a week or more. Many major corporations spend up to $600,000 a year for recruitment ads.

Besides their concern over wasting hard-earned profits, companies are haunted by other problems that advertising can introduce. Image and security, for example. By announcing a chronic need for new chemists, Du Pont may be signaling their competition that they are on the eve of a serious new-product development program. When Xerox calls for résumés from experienced salesmen, this could be interpreted as an attempt to crush the competitive inroads made by smaller manufacturers. Employers are also nervous over the effects these ads may have internally. When General Foods advertises for senior product managers, you can just imagine what is going through the minds of GF's assistant product managers.

With just one call for help, corporations can expose themselves to innumerable crackpots, lawsuits or embarrassing and time-consuming events. If Boeing were to advertise for welders today, it is a safe bet that several totally unqualified applicants would attempt to use this opportunity to force themselves down the giant employer's throat. A double amputee, for example, might claim that he can weld with his feet. By taking the case to court, he could cost Boeing $50,000 in legal fees and paralyze the hiring process for many months. The more common claims of racial or sexual discrimination cost America's corporations untold millions each year and are an engraved invitation to the federal government to begin interfering directly in the company's hiring policies.

But don't begin to assume that Help Wanted ads are totally without value. They sometimes lead to productive interviews and are often an important source of vital information.

If you haven't already done so, start to build a substan-

tial file of advertisements that intrigue you. Spread them
all out on your desk and begin to study each one carefully.
BUT DON'T ANSWER THEM!

Examine the language. Remember that the person who
wrote the ad has spelled out his "ideal" candidate. Very
often this is some utopian character who doesn't exist
or who, in many cases, is not the best person for the
job. Don't become discouraged when this "ideal" person
doesn't match your profile. Naturally, you would not
qualify for a position as a legal assistant if you had absolutely no background in the law. But just because the ad
says "law degree desired" or "litigation experience preferred," this doesn't rule you out. Your experience in real
estate, for example, may make you just the person that ad
is trying to attract.

Don't let a low salary figure turn you off. Consider it
the beginning of salary negotiations at the very least. You
can bet that the employer has a firm idea of the maximum
salary he can afford and you can also bet that he is clever
enough not to advertise that figure.

Age and sex are also a statement of the employer's
"ideal." Even though it is now illegal to discriminate
against employees on these qualifications, don't rule
yourself out even if you sense he prefers someone you are
not. A company looking for a "mature candidate" is interested in men and women over forty. But with perseverance, there is no reason why a qualified thirty-year-old
can't wangle an interview and win it.

But what should you do when you discover an advertisement that is so perfect, so enticing that it practically
asks for you by name? Should you immediately send
them your résumé? *Absolutely not!* Should you give them a

call? *Never.* If you use your head, they will discover you all by themselves. At least they think they will. Here's why. While dozens, perhaps hundreds of job-hungry people are flooding the employer's mailbox with letters and résumés, you will have contacted the company *independently,* as though you were totally unaware that it was advertising at all. Because you have done your homework, you already know the name of the person who will make the actual hiring decision. And while everyone else is begging the personnel officer to be considered, your candidacy is receiving special consideration, as though you were the grandson of the chairman of the board!

Oh yes, your letter may very well get routed to the personnel person who placed the ad. But suddenly you're out in front of the pack. You have gained a powerful ally within the company who is seriously interested in your case. No personnel officer who values his career can afford to ignore a suggestion by one of his superiors.

And because you know a job opening exists (something you *never* acknowledge), you are in a position to play into the employer's hands without its ever being known. You have the confidence to control the interview situation. You know where to begin salary negotiations. You can ask piercing questions and provide intelligent answers. In short, you know where the interview is leading while they're still playing games. And most important, you are not just another groveling job seeker. You are an informed, highly selective individual who has flattered the company by recognizing its merits independently—without having been seduced by advertising.

Many Help Wanted ads are "blind." Instead of indicating the name of the company at the bottom of the ad, they provide some vague description of the company's operation. All responses are directed to a newspaper or magazine box number, so that the applicant usually has no idea which company is seducing him. This infuriating and increasingly popular gimmick can be cracked. Indeed, you *must* crack it if you are to be successful.

In many cases simple common sense will tell you which company it is. The description of its product or service, the size of the company, the coincidence of the advertisement with news you may have heard, strange requirements common to a particular corporation . . . these kinds of things can be very big hints. An advertisement for a specialized technical position "with a division of a major business machine company in Ann Arbor, Michigan" can only mean one thing . . . a job with University Microfilms, a division of Xerox. After all, how many "major business machine" companies have a branch in Ann Arbor?

Some blind ads, of course, are more difficult. One popular underground technique involves using a third person. Simply enlist a friend or acquaintance with absolutely superior credentials and send his résumé in to the box number. Once you have established the company's identity, proceed according to your own plan.

Some applicants invent a fictitious character complete with a glowing résumé. Others have had success sending out empty envelopes by registered mail. By examining the return receipt from the registered letter, it is often possible to discover not only the name of the company in question but also the full name of the actual interviewer!

Finally, what about job hunters who advertise themselves? This idea may have occurred to you independently or you may have seen it done. My advice is, watch out! Employers rarely read this advertising and almost never take it seriously. If you place one of these ads, you'll get discovered, all right. You'll hear from third-rate employment agencies, various merchants whose products you can live without, and dubious characters filled with nasty tricks that only spell trouble.

BEWARE OF THE TELEPHONE

Many years ago I remember accepting a bet that I would be able to speak to Henry Ford II, chairman of the Ford Motor Company, America's third largest corporation. Having just read that Mr. Ford was attending an honorary dinner at the Waldorf-Astoria Hotel that evening, I immediately called the hotel asking to be put through as his son. In a matter of seconds I found myself talking with a very angry billionaire.

I am continually amazed at how a single telephone call commands the kind of attention that a letter, telegram or even a 200-piece marching band could never muster. All of us regularly permit phone calls to interrupt our personal conversations, meetings, sleep, thought, even love-making. With only a modicum of ingenuity you will have no trouble bringing anyone to the telephone, including the President of the United States. But beware!

It has been said that for job seekers the telephone is best used for *gathering information, not dishing it out.* I concur. So, before you pick up the receiver, ask yourself if perhaps your cause might be better served with a letter. The chances are that it will, 95 percent of the time.

However, there are exceptions. In a fast-breaking situation where time is of the essence, the telephone may be your only answer. Thirteen years ago, in an act of blind rage, I quit a job over a matter of policy and left the office moments later. Out on the street, suddenly realizing what I had done, I telephoned some professional aides on Bobby Kennedy's presidential-primary staff. That afternoon I flew from New York to Indiana, where I immediately assumed local command of Mr. Kennedy's campaign promotion. In that particular case, if I had waited a few more hours or had left my fate to a letter and résumé, I would have been out of luck.

When a company has an immediate, publicized need for help, a telephone call is very much in order. Or if you have good reason to feel that your call would be welcome, don't hesitate. But if you are considering using the telephone simply to arrange an interview, forget it. One unwelcome call can instantly seal off valuable opportunities with a permanent wall of animosity. One applicant I know called an executive at Nationwide Insurance Company telling his secretary that the call was urgent and personal. Knowing that her boss was going through a family crisis, the secretary pulled him out of an important meeting. When the executive discovered that it was not the surgeon calling, guess who was out of an interview and a possible job?

If you are absolutely convinced that the telephone offers you the best avenue to approach the man who is going to hire you, there are several things you must remember:

Always know whom you are calling. Just as you would never write a blind letter to a company, never call without knowing the person's full name. You can use company operators to find out names and accurate spelling for follow-up letters. For higher-level jobs, it may be helpful to have your secretary put the call through for you.

Do not tell his secretary the call is personal. You'll get connected, all right, but the person on the other end will resent your invasion of his privacy and find it difficult to forgive you. Anyone who feels tricked into accepting your call will be skeptical about anything else you say.

An effective end run around secretaries and assistants is to call before 9 A.M. or after 5 P.M. Most secretaries work 9 to 5, give or take a few seconds. And an early or late call usually catches executives answering their own phones. An excellent opportunity.

Offer something special to the person you're calling. What you say in the first few seconds of your call determines just how successful you will be. Offering your availability for hire or rattling off your credentials is an immediate turn-off. This permits the person you are calling to respond with a quick and final "No thanks."

Instead, give him a reason to hear you out. Make him curious. Give him some news that he will value. Asking him if you can come in for an interview is a giant yawn. Telling him that you have an interesting theory on why his package design isn't working is real news.

HEADHUNTERS, BODY SNATCHERS, CAMPUS INTERVIEWERS AND MEAT RACKS

It is always more exciting to discover someone and fall in love than to settle for an arranged marriage. And whether they say so or not, most executives feel this way too. If they feel they have discovered you or that you have independently sought them out above all others, they tend to take you more seriously. However, this isn't always possible.

Approximately 15 percent of all job placements each year are funneled through middlemen of one type or another. Private, state and federal employment agencies handle the bulk of these placements. Executive recruiters and management consultants deal in significantly smaller numbers but bigger salaries.

Private employment agencies, better known as "flesh peddlers" or "headhunters," certainly must rank as one of the most maligned groups on earth. Numbering more than 10,000 coast to coast, these brokers earn their living by introducing job hunters to employers and collecting a fee for their services.

For corporations, these agencies offer immediate and easy access to a pool of talented labor while insulating them from the hordes of unqualified applicants just waiting to beat down the company gates.

For you, private employment agencies may sometimes be a source of quality job interviews. Please note I said interviews, not jobs. *No headhunter ever got anybody hired.* You must do that by winning your interview.

Choosing the best employment agency is more difficult than it first appears. There are good ones, there are gangsters, and a lot of dreary folk in between. You should only sign on with the top agencies. That means spending a couple of hours of investigative time asking friends and acquaintances while steering clear of the Yellow Pages. Which agencies *specialize* in the kind of job you are after? You may want to call the companies you would like to work for. Ask *them* which agency they use. Then visit that agency, being certain to tell them the name of the company and the individual that recommended them. This will earn you special attention. The last thing any headhunter needs is a bad reputation in dealing with a good applicant.

What kind of *track record* does a particular agency have? Find out by calling the Better Business Bureau or talking to people who have firsthand experience. Check newspaper ads to see what kind of jobs the agency offers. Are these jobs filled regularly or do they go begging for months? If you catch an agency advertising jobs that don't exist, report it to the state authorities and avoid it at all costs. That cruel trick is against the law in most states.

Who pays the fee? Today most fees, *but not all,* are paid by the employer. Usually it is a percentage of your first year's salary, somewhere between 10 and 25 percent. If the employer pays the fee, this is good news for your bank account, but there is one big hitch. Your headhunter's true loyalty is not with you, it's with your interviewer. Many job hunters refuse to accept this fact and live to regret it. Employment agencies ask all job hunters to sign a short contract outlining fees and other agreements. Read that contract carefully *before* you sign on.

During your first meeting with the agency, find out exactly what they plan to do for you. Don't just dump yourself into their lap. Make sure that you agree with everything they recommend. Every headhunter has difficult-to-fill jobs that he tries to unload on naïve applicants. Don't fall into this trap no matter how desperate you think you are. The last thing you need is a job that isn't exactly what you want.

Headhunters have a rotten habit of passing themselves

off as authorities on the employment picture. More often than not, their information is way out of tune, as most employers will quickly tell you. They are authorities on only one thing: getting warm bodies into company reception rooms. If you want a job as an investment adviser, for example, don't let them convince you that the field has dried up. If you have done your homework, the chances are excellent that you know more about your field of interest than any headhunter.

I have always believed that under ideal circumstances, the dedicated and serious job seeker would be better served if the headhunter revealed the company that needed help, the name of the interviewer and then quietly drop out of the picture. Of course, not only would this make the agency people scream bloody murder, it is illegal and shouldn't be attempted. However, there is no reason why you can't follow up on leads that other people have developed. In fact, if you should ever have this opportunity, leap at it.

Many private employment agencies try to get their customers to sign up exclusively with them. This is a reasonable request considering the fact that good agencies will invest a significant number of man-hours getting to know you, your qualifications and your specific demands. And there can be no question that they will take you more seriously if they know you are not playing one agency against another. If, however, after ten days your agency has produced zero interviews or dead-end interviews, jump to another agency. Immediately.

When you are faced with the decision to accept or decline a particular job offer, the last piece of advice you need is from your headhunter. He may have your best interests at heart. But the odds are against it. Why? Remember, he collects his fee the day you go to work. Not a second before. And from his point of view, the sooner the better. So take your time. Rush into nothing. And when in doubt, ask him to set up more interviews.

"Body snatchers," referred to professionally as executive recruiters, search firms or development specialists, are another kind of animal, never to be confused with private employment agencies. An increasing number of corporations hire these firms, usually on an annual retainer fee, to fill a specified number of openings that call for highly trained or specialized individuals. Nationally, these firms may handle only a tiny fraction of the job placements, but they receive the cream of the crop. Typically they are used for upper-level management jobs paying over $25,000. Often they specialize in hard-to-locate professionals: an accountant who speaks fluent Bulgarian or a senior geologist willing to take up residence on an oil platform off Taiwan.

Search/recruitment firms enjoy a special relationship with their corporate clients, unheard of among headhunters. They are more informed about their clients, their clients' needs, personalities and idiosyncrasies. They work in an atmosphere of trust and cooperation. Some companies share their deepest secrets with their executive recruiter. A large number of corporations do virtually all their hiring through these firms.

All body snatchers maintain voluminous files and contacts within their area of expertise. Once given an assignment, they burn up the telephone lines trying to tempt successfully employed people to consider changing jobs. Hence the name "body snatcher."

Those fresh out of school or currently unemployed should waste little time considering these recruiters. These firms want people with proven track records. You may be perfectly qualified for the jobs they are offering, but in the interest of your time you will have to approach the employer through other channels. Don't despair if your phone hasn't been jangling with hungry body snatchers on the other end of the line.

However, if you are currently employed, you may wish to make your name known to them. This is a job that calls for the diplomacy of a royal courtship. Letters, résumés and phone calls are not your best avenue of approach. Letting them "discover" you is the trick. Many hyperaggressive executives and professionals make a concerted effort to get their names inserted into professional journals and newspapers, just to flag down body snatchers. Listings in *Who's Who* and other compilations are also helpful. But a far simpler and more time-efficient method is to have other people "volunteer" your name to the search firm. To significantly increase the likelihood of this event, put the word out among people you know in the business that interests you. Make sure your name is on the tip of their tongue the day the body snatcher calls *them.*

An interview with an executive recruitment firm should receive the same serious attention and preparation you would give to the employer himself. Clarence E. McFeely, of McFeely, Wackerle Associates, tells us, "The duration of the average search is at least three months." This means his firm and others spend ninety days searching out qualified candidates and subjecting each one to several in-depth interviews and reference checks. They may want to meet your spouse or talk to an old boss. They will go to remarkable lengths before they dare approach an employer with a recommendation.

Indeed, body snatchers are a rich and growing source of quality, high-paying jobs. *Business Week* has reported that "recruitment assignments were up 20%." But how your name gets into their files and how you carry yourself during their exhaustive interviews is crucially important.

Both undergraduate and graduate students have numerous opportunities to obtain interview experience and, often, excellent jobs before they graduate. I am referring, of course, to the campus interviews conducted by major corporations. And no one who has this opportunity should fail to take full advantage of it. Most of these companies are offering career-enriching training programs that are the launching pad for the next generation of corporate executives.

It is imperative that you understand how these campus interviews have changed in today's tightening and specialized job market. No longer are recruiters looking for just the bright, well-groomed students they snapped up during the sixties. Today they are demanding more, and you should be prepared to give more. Choose your interviews carefully. Do your homework thoroughly.

The interviewers themselves are a tough, cynical lot. They meet an awesome number of students each week, and in the process they develop a snap-judgment technique which you must be aware of. As one particularly candid recruiter from a large package-goods company told me, "My decision is ninety percent made once I've scanned his [a student's] transcript and had a few seconds to look him over. Nothing makes me angrier than these smart-asses who come in thinking we owe them a job when they don't have the slightest idea of what we do or how we performed last quarter."

Laid-back students who view these recruiters as corporate weaklings with virtually no power to make the hiring decision are making a terrible mistake. Unless they can sufficiently impress this individual, any further progress along the interviewing trail is hopeless.

The state and federal employment services, sometimes referred to as "meat racks," handle the largest number of job placements each year. Their services are free, and the majority of their listings are blue-collar and lower-paying white-collar jobs. However, on rare occasions they may have listings for $15,000 or more.

For the highly motivated job seeker, government employment services provide little in the way of promising opportunities. If all you want is a job, no doubt you will find one here quickly. But if you are insisting on a job with genuine growth potential and a salary that is commensurate, you may be disappointed.

THREE

How to Answer the Questions Your New Boss Will Ask You

General questions for all job hunters

Questions for those currently employed or between jobs

Questions for recent graduates just entering the job market

S EVERAL days before every press conference, members of President Reagan's staff compile a list of every conceivable question that might be asked. They then formulate a well-worded response to each one. The President studies the answers carefully, committing the content and sometimes the exact language to memory. He knows that he must not be caught by surprise. He must appear knowledgeable and concerned about *all* issues. He must disarm hostile reporters with his confidence and preparation. He knows that the second he starts to answer questions off the top of his head, he is in big trouble.

Most job hunters make two devastating mistakes when they are being questioned in an interview. First, they fail to *listen* to the question. They proceed to annoy the interviewer either by answering a question that wasn't asked or by giving out a lot of superfluous nonsense.

Second, and most important, they attempt to answer questions with virtually *no preparation.* The glibbest person on earth, even the most skilled debater, cannot answer questions off the cuff without damaging his chances of success. ITT's Harold Geneen used to tell job hunters, "I'm not asking questions, I'm waiting for answers!" You

can have these answers if you take the trouble to anticipate the questions and prepare your responses.

What follows is a number of questions that various
surveys have indicated are asked most often, regardless of
the job classification. Study all of these questions carefully, develop strong responses, and your candidacy will
receive prime consideration.

GENERAL QUESTIONS FOR ALL JOB HUNTERS

1. "Why should I hire you?"

The interviewer asking this question does not want a
lengthy regurgitation of what your résumé has already
told him. He is not yet asking for a barrage of facts and
figures. He is interested in testing your poise and confidence. Give him a *short, generalized summary.* "I have the
qualifications to do the job that has to be done, and my
track record proves it." If you are younger: "I am capable of quickly learning what you have to teach me and
I can be productive in a short amount of time." Or: "I've
chosen this field [your business] after a considerable
amount of in-depth investigation and personal evaluation. I know that this is the job for me and that I will be
successful."

2. "Why do you want to work here?"

This should be your easiest and favorite question to
answer. In fact, if he doesn't ask it, volunteer the information anyway. Because you have done your homework on
his company, you *know* exactly why you want to work
there. All you must do is organize your reasons into sev-

eral short, hard-hitting sentences. Using *facts, not puffery,* tell him why his company is your number-one choice. For example, "You make the best product on the market today. You've got a sales force that is aggressive and imaginative. Your management is far-sighted enough to reinvest profits so that soon you will be the leader in the category."

3. "What interests you most about this position?"

Here's a perfect chance to tease your interviewer's curiosity. Give him a truthful one- or two-word answer like "The future" . . . "The challenge" . . . "The competitiveness" . . . "The environment." This response will force the employer to ask you to explain, giving you yet another opportunity to demonstrate your profound knowledge of his company.

4. "Would you like to have your boss's job?"

By all means, "Yes!" Ambitious, hungry people are always preferred over those willing to settle for a safe routine. If you sense this answer may be too arrogant or threatens your interviewer's security, you might add, "when I am judged qualified" or "should an opening develop in several years."

5. "Are you willing to go where the company sends you?"

Obviously, this is being asked because they have every intention of shipping you off. If you answer "no," you will probably not be hired. If you answer "yes," understand that once you are a trusted employee you will be able to exert the necessary leverage to avoid the less desirable out-of-town assignments.

6. "What causes you to lose your temper?"

Everybody has a low boiling point on some particular issue. Pick one of yours, something relatively safe, reasonable and inconsequential: "People who are late to meetings." "Obvious lying." "Lazy colleagues." Don't try out for sainthood by saying you never fly off the handle. You'll lose.

7. "Who has had the greatest influence on you?"

Give one name. A person with some authority: a professor in school, an old boss, an author, etc. Then be prepared to give a very short explanation: "He taught me to be unafraid of new ideas. She showed me how to focus on what really matters."

8. "Do you have any health problems?"

Tell the truth. Summarize everything in one sentence. If he wants to know more, he'll ask. "I'm in perfect health now, although I was treated for a prostatic condition several years ago." "Everything is fine except the vision in my right eye."

9. "What kind of decisions are most difficult for you?"

Once again, be human and admit that not everything comes easy. But be careful what you do admit. Make sure you are not instantly disqualifying yourself. "I find it difficult to decide which of two good men [women] must be let go." "It is difficult for me to tell a client that he is running his business badly."

10. "How do you feel about your progress to date?"

Never apologize for yourself. You can't expect someone to hire you if you don't think highly of your own capabilities and accomplishments. "I think I've done well, but I need new challenges and opportunities." This is a good time to drop hero stories: "No one in my company has advanced as fast as I have." "I think you'll agree, I've accomplished quite a bit in the last five years."

11. *"How long will you stay with the company?"*

As with marriage, most employers expect a "till death do us part" attitude. But they are equally attracted to someone with a combination of ambition and candor. A reasonable response might be, "as long as I continue to learn and grow in my field."

12. *"What are your greatest accomplishments?"*

Be ready to deliver one or two short hero stories that demonstrate some capability which will make you attractive to your new employer. If you are fresh out of school, consider an academic experience or something connected with summer employment.

13. *"Whom can we check as references?"*

Be ready with a neatly typed list of four or five individuals who are willing to recommend you highly. Ideally, it is best to offer references from various areas: business, academic, civic, etc. Your eagerness and preparation will impress your interviewer.

14. *"Do you have plans to continue your studies?"*

You must know the employer to be able to answer this question effectively. If you are applying for a job where an advanced degree is important if not necessary, and if you honestly intend to take evening classes, by all means tell your interviewer. In fact, tell him the precise degree you'll be working toward, the classes you'll be attending and, if possible, the names of the professors. Your command of these details will convince the interviewer of your dedication and sincerity. On the other hand, beware of employers who question the value of additional education. Your ambition may signal that you will not be with their company very long.

15. "How do you feel about a male/female boss?"

Count on the fact that your new boss will be of the opposite sex. And be certain that if you register any concern, you will not be hired.

16. "Have you done the best work of which you are capable?"

This Boy Scout question is best answered with some degree of self-effacement. "I would be lying to you if I told you I was perfect, but I have tackled every assignment with all my energy and talents." Or: "I'm sure there were times when I could have worked harder or longer, but over the years I've tried to do my best and I believe I have succeeded."

17. "What would you like to be doing five years from now?"

To answer this question, make sure you know exactly what can and cannot be achieved by the ideal candidate in your shoes. Too many job hunters butcher this question because they have not done their homework and have no idea where their career will lead them. If you see yourself at another company, or in another department of the present company, tread lightly. You can't afford to tell your interviewer that you believe you'll be more successful than he is.

18. "What training/qualifications do you have for a job like this?"

Your interviewer could probably answer this question himself after looking at your résumé. But he wants to hear you explain in person, so don't give him a rehash. Deliver a short, fact-filled summary of the two or three most important qualifications you have: "I have a background in accounting. I've demonstrated proven selling skills. I'm capable of handling several projects simultaneously." If you are a recent graduate, try to construct an answer that includes both academic and job-related experiences.

19. "Do you have any questions?"

"Absolutely!" See Chapter 9 for a suggested list of important questions you must ask.

QUESTIONS FOR THOSE CURRENTLY EMPLOYED OR BETWEEN JOBS

1. "Why do you want to change jobs?"

This is one of the first questions interviewers ask. Be ready to answer it with a carefully rehearsed speech which your interviewer will find both believable and completely understandable. If you're currently in a dead-end position, locked out of advancement opportunities, explain this to him. He'll understand. If your job has become a routine, void of learning experiences, he'll accept that explanation and sympathize. If you feel your present employer is losing ground to competition, through no fault of your own, he'll accept that, too.

But if you tell him that your salary is too low, he'll become suspicious. If you tell him you hate your boss, he'll get nervous, wondering if soon you'll be hating him.

If you tell him you are bored, he'll suspect that you're just another job hopper.

2. *"Why do you want to change your field of work?"*

No doubt you have several solid reasons for wanting to change careers. Before your interview, spend one hour and organize these reasons into a written statement. Memorize this explanation and be prepared to deliver it, because you will certainly be asked. Your explanation should include the following:

a. How your previous work experience will contribute to your new career.

b. What excites you most about this new field.

c. How you came to make this career-change decision.

3. *"Why were you out of work for so long?"*

If there is a gap in your résumé, you must be prepared to explain what you were doing in that period. Until you have satisfied your interviewer's curiosity you will not get hired. If you were fired and have spent the last year looking for a job without success, you will understand an employer's reluctance to hire you. If, on the other hand, you explain what you have learned or accomplished during this hiatus, he will warm to your candidacy. For example, "I have taken several courses to strengthen my skills in . . ." Or: "I used this period to re-examine my goals and have reached this conclusion: . . ." The interviewer needs a positive explanation *from* you before he can think positively *about* you.

4. *"Why will this job be any different from others you have held?"*

This is just another version of Question #1. Answer it positively, and be sure to include aspects of this new position which were not present in other jobs. If you sense that your interviewer suspects that you are a job switcher, you must be sure to calm his fears.

5. "Why have you changed jobs so frequently?"

This is a very serious question. In fact, it is one of the top reasons why applicants fail to get the jobs they want. You must answer this question to your interviewer's complete satisfaction. You must convince him that your job-hopping days are over. If you feel you made a mistake leaving previous jobs, tell him so, while at the same time reminding him that your job performance was never in question. He'll appreciate your candor. If something in your personal or business life has recently changed and would affect your stability in the future. . . . come out with the facts. He'll be anxious to hear.

6. "Have you ever hired or fired anyone?"

You are being asked this question for two important reasons. First, he wants to determine whether you are capable of performing these duties. Second, he is doing a bit of investigation. He is trying to determine if the previous experience you have described to him was at a high enough level to include hiring/firing responsibility. If you have had no experience in hiring/firing, you must make a considerable effort to convince him that you are capable of performing in this area.

7. "How have you helped sales/profits/cost reductions?"

Have your hero stories ready and be willing to prove to him that you have made significant contributions in one or more of these basic areas. Again, keep your explanations short and try to include specific dollar amounts.

Invite him to contact references or other individuals who can corroborate your story.

8. *"Why aren't you earning more at your age?"*

This question, a current favorite, can frighten the wits out of an unsuspecting applicant. One of the following suggested responses should cover your situation:

"I have been willing to sacrifice short-term earnings because I felt that I was gaining valuable experience."

"I have received (been promised) company stock (or other benefits) in lieu of an increase in salary."

"I have been reluctant to gain a reputation as a job-hopper, preferring instead to build my career on solid, long-term achievement."

9. *"How many people have you supervised?"*

Similar to the "hired or fired" question, the interviewer is trying to determine the depth of your experience. Be careful not to exaggerate. If you've never been in a supervisory position but aspire to be, demonstrate your expertise at delegating or coordinating work. For example, "I am in charge of assigning all projects in the research group." Or: "I am responsible for evaluating fifteen people in my department." "I am always consulted on the technical accuracy of contracts our salesmen produce."

10. *"What are the reasons for your success?"*

It is best to keep this answer very general, permitting your interviewer to probe deeper if he wishes. Offer him a short list of positive character traits that describe you:

"I like to work hard." Or: "I get along with all kinds of people and I know how to listen." Or: "I pay close attention to details, I know how to watch costs and I can keep difficult customers smiling."

11. "Does your present employer know that you're looking?"
Tell the truth. But understand beforehand that your candidacy will receive more serious attention if your interviewer thinks he has to lure you away.

12. "What kind of experience do you have for this job?"
Summarize four or five key areas of experience which you can bring to your new job. Demonstrate to him specifically how each one helps solve *his* problems. For example, "My experience in new-product introductions will be very helpful to your entire marketing effort." "My industrial design background will strengthen your sales-force capability in dealing with large clients."

QUESTIONS FOR RECENT GRADUATES JUST ENTERING THE JOB MARKET

1. "Why do you want to enter this particular field?"
Naïve or superficial answers to this question are unacceptable. You must be able to deliver a carefully reasoned response which is based on fact. You must demonstrate to your interviewer that you know what you are talking about. "I am interested in financial management because I know that the corporate leaders of the future will probably be chosen from this area." You may want to bring your aptitudes and academic background into the answer:

"I love working with figures, have done well in all math courses and I am especially intrigued with statistical work." You may want to cite early experiences: "I've wanted to be in the newspaper business since I was nine years old. I guess it was my father who turned me on to it."

2. *"What honors did you earn?"*

Easy question if you have any. Pure torture if you don't and are unprepared. In the latter situation, *do not* shrink into your shell. Don't make excuses. Don't acknowledge failure. Don't be negative. Come on strong and positive. Be ready to deliver convincing evidence of your abilities. True, you may have to reach a bit, but your enthusiasm can save the day.

If you were a class officer or a member of any academic societies, let him know it. If a particular thesis or paper received special acclaim, if you took unusual courses related to his business, if you have interesting hero stories about school/summer employment . . . this is the time to get the news out. Comb through your last three years and develop a list of experiences, awards, special achievements, endorsements, citations, anything that might be at all meaningful to your interviewer. But do this *before* you step into his office. You'll never be able to develop this list on the spot.

3. *"What is your primary interest? Money, power, prestige, etc.?"*

This question is another trap. Don't fall into it. Don't let a lazy interviewer typecast you before he gets a chance to know you. If you acknowledge that money, power or prestige are paramount in your plan for the future, most interviewers will write you off as greedy, one-dimensional and naïve. As a beginner you can only have one primary interest: to learn and develop valuable skills that will lead you to a career filled with opportunies, challenges and, ultimately, rewards.

4. *"How would a friend who knows you well describe you?"*
You must have a short one- or two-sentence answer. But before you deliver this answer to your interviewer, pause a few minutes in thought. Give your interviewer the impression that he has really put you on the spot. Then deliver your prepared statement, being especially careful to use fresh, exciting language, denuded of clichés. For example, "Pete would rather read the *Wall Street Journal* than *Playboy.*" "Sally could sell Bibles to the Godfather." "George simply doesn't know how to lie."

5. *"Would you rather work with words than figures?"*
Usually the kind of job you are after will dictate your response. An aspiring accountant who would rather work with words is in big trouble. But there are millions of jobs that demand skills in both areas. And you will have to tiptoe carefully, indicating that you are comfortable working with words and figures. Only after you have made that point very clear can you answer his question directly.

6. *"What courses did you like best?"*
Before you answer this question, ask yourself what your answer will reveal about you. A research chemist who tells his interviewer that his favorite course was Eliz-

abethan poetry is making a fundamental mistake. He would be better served to qualify his response, "My favorite *chemistry* course was . . ." On the other hand, a liberal arts major applying for a job in sales, advertising or media-related industries might be well served to excite his interviewer's curiosity by revealing his breadth of interests: "I especially enjoyed Russian literature and, curiously enough, geology."

7. "Which school activities did you participate in?"

Interviewers ask this question to help round out the perception they have of you. The worst mistake you can make is admit you were not involved in any meaningful activities. The best you can do is reveal activities that might complement the job you are looking for: Debating Team, Economics Club, political or international affairs groups, etc.

8. "What books have you read in the last month? Did you see any movies? Plays?"

Are you a person who gets excited by new ideas? Do you enjoy reading, or do you prefer your entertainment delivered on a television screen? Are you intellectually curious? These are a few of the things interviewers want to know about you. Deliver your answers with enthusiasm. Try to pique *his* interest in your recent favorites. This mutual enthusiasm can do wonders for the interpersonal chemistry so important in all interviews.

9. "How would you describe success?"

With this type of question it is best not to get specific. In most interviews you will be best served by saving specific answers for specific questions. Avoid being stereotyped and pigeonholed into one of your interviewer's classifications with a general answer like "Success is doing the best you can with your given potential."

10. "How long will it take you to make a contribution to this company?"

Watch out! This question can get you into big trouble. Some jobs require months, even years, of training. And a cocky pronouncement that you will immediately be productive will only reveal your ignorance. Make sure you understand the length of the learning period ahead of you before you give an answer.

FOUR

Forget Your Leisure Suit, but Not Your Bra

Your age . . . too old?
Too young?

I T is indeed tempting to tell you that how you look, dress and smell is of no real importance. That you should look and act in a way that feels most comfortable. That your true character and qualifications will rise above surface impressions and make the ultimate decision. It is all tempting to say, but wrong, wrong, wrong!

For someone meeting you for the first time, and hopefully not the last, *your appearance says more about you than anything you can say about yourself.* In fact, long after you have left your interviewer's office this physical impression will stick in his mind. Make it positive.

C. Peter McColough, the outspoken chairman of Xerox, has much to say while grappling with this difficult subject. "I'm turned away by a lack of manners. Manners essentially is concern for others. I suppose extremes of dress affect me negatively [as well]. Since dress is not the reason we've met, why intrude its obvious presence, whether too conservative or too fashionable?

"Certain people have a leadership look that appeals to me," McColough continues. "It's difficult to describe. But I guess it's an above-surface glimpse of their character and personality. You generally know when you see it; those who have it are people other people will follow."

Forbes magazine, writing about William Paley, former chairman of CBS, reported that job prospects knew they "would be judged not only on their administrative skills, but also on their grammar, their clothes and, indeed, even on the way they parted their hair. Paley is notorious for measuring a man by the width of his lapels . . . an executive was once sent home to change his Argyle socks."

It is impossible to calculate, and not one interviewer in a thousand would dare 'fess up, but it is my firm opinion that a person's appearance is the single most common weapon employers use to reduce the number of prospects under consideration. Xerox's McColough says, "Appearance is important only if it indicates a lack of discipline, as in sloppiness or extreme overweight."

Dozens of studies have confirmed what most of us would naturally suspect: that physically attractive men and women stand a better chance of being hired. No one, of course, would suggest plastic surgery as a preliminary step to interviews. But it is reasonable to ask applicants to make the very most of what they have.

Because what you wear is the most effective way to enhance your appearance, it is vitally important that you give your interviewing wardrobe careful thought. Bearing in mind the business that interests you, make sure you look like the kind of person "the power" wants to promote. If your clothes are significantly different from the interviewer's, you are instantly handing him the excuse he needs to begin doubting your other qualifications.

In many cases you may be well advised to make a serious investment in your appearance. A couple of hundred dollars invested today in a new suit or dress may pay off immediately with a salary thousands of dollars higher than you were prepared to accept. Your appearance may even suggest to an employer that you are perhaps qualified for an even more responsible position.

The self-appointed authority John T. Molloy, author of *The Men's Dress for Success Book* and *The Women's Dress for Success Book,* offers some valuable insights into the importance of dress. "Most men," notes Molloy, "dress for failure. The most common mistake they make is letting their wives, girl friends or sales clerks influence their apparel." Suits are the positive authority symbol. The darker the suit, the more authority. Dark blue and dark gray with or without pin stripes exude credibility. When you want to be liked, wear light gray, light blue or medium-ranged plaids.

Molloy does not recommend sports coats for interviews. And a very interesting survey conducted by some Stanford University graduate students confirms his opinion. "As far as appearance is concerned, a male applicant makes a mildly positive impression in a sports coat and slacks, but he makes a stronger impression in a suit." This same survey, conducted among 100 personnel recruiters from seventeen different industries (industries that have hired more than 75 percent of all college graduates since 1972), indicates that college students who shun traditional job-hunting attire have the cards stacked heavily against them.

Your weight, height and general physical build should receive thorough consideration. Very large men who wear dark pin-stripe suits often appear overpowering and dictatorial. Lighter colors would help them appear more amiable and flexible. The opposite, of course, applies to small men who must convince an employer that they are "big enough" for the job in question.

Coast to coast, virtually all interviewers agree that men should wear a necktie, a minimum of jewelry, long dark-colored socks and a white shirt. If you find yourself resenting this suggestion, you have my sympathy but not my tolerance. Years of tradition have prescribed this small bit of conformity. And while you may ignore it freely, do so at your own risk. Just because you are wearing a shark's tooth or a gold-plated razor blade around your neck doesn't mean you aren't capable of managing a forty-man sales force. But ask yourself this question: Would I hand over my life's savings to a banker dressed in Bermuda shorts and a fishnet T-shirt?

If you don't have one, get yourself a long-sleeved white cotton dress shirt. Synthetic materials continue to suggest that there is perhaps something synthetic about the person wearing them. Short sleeves, even in hot climates, suggest leisure, not hard work.

Nobody is asking you to forsake your favorite necktie. But how will it serve you in an interview? Molloy explains: "If you think it's your car, house or size of your bank account that is significant to success, you're wrong. It's your tie. It's the symbol of respectability. So choose it carefully. Even if it hurts, spend as much as $18. Conservatively colored paisley, polka-dot or solid ties made of silk are ideal. The width should match the width of your lapel."

In a statement about success that many now find amusing, Aristotle Onassis once suggested that ambitious men "keep a tan in winter; to most people sun is money . . . live at a good address even if you have to live in a room in the attic." This idea may be dated, but the spirit is right on. How you dress and present yourself will accomplish the same goal in an age when suntans often connote laziness and fancy addresses spell inherited money.

Most women bristle at the suggestion that their own taste in clothes may not serve them well in an interview. Molloy suggests that women adopt a business "uniform" for success—a dark skirted suit and a light contrasting blouse. He recommends full-cut jackets, long sleeves, skirts just below the knee. He hates vests, sweaters, pastel colors, clingy fabrics and pantsuits—stating they are unprofessional and lack authority. Carol Drewry, former supervisor of employment at Holiday Inns, retorts acidly, "I think Molloy's philosophy is too rigid. I prefer a business look that incorporates my femininity rather than having a business uniform. I find that dresses, skirts and blouses can serve the same purpose."

Barbara Walters is quite vocal on the same subject. "Play it safe when you dress," she cautions. "Wear stockings; don't wear pantsuits. Go easy on the makeup and perfume and hairdo. Be clean—if you can't decide whether or not a dress looks fresh enough to wear one more time, it doesn't."

Women run into a major problem whenever their appearance can be interpreted as being sexy. Barbara Walters advises: "Be sexy on your own time; working hours and job interviews require the crisp and cool version of you. Employment offices agree that the beddable look does not lead to the *door marked President but to the one marked Exit.*"

Any woman looking for a job who lets the fashion industry dictate her wardrobe is certainly looking for trouble. Female fashion is not designed for or accepted by the business world. A woman across an interviewer's desk must exude confidence and authority.

A lot of nonsense has been written on the subject of jewelry, perfume and various accessories. Most people agree: less is best. With one major exception—a briefcase. Taken for granted among men, the briefcase is the quickest and easiest method for a woman to telegraph her authority and seriousness. It is the only visible symbol you have that will immediately separate you from millions of housewives. Carry one, use it, make it part of your interview.

YOUR AGE . . . TOO OLD? TOO YOUNG?

In the panic and insecurity that too often accompany job hunting, many people seem to actually enjoy finding excuses why they are unqualified for a particular job. Being too old or too young is a favorite phobia, exaggerated beyond reasonableness.

The over-forty terror that seems to have gripped a large segment of the job-hunting population is a classic example. Yes, it is true that fifty-year-olds are not welcome in most training programs. But the majority of job openings can be filled by older people if they concentrate on *selling their experience* and maturity instead of hiding it.

Part of this endeavor is to stop trying to act and dress as though you were just entering puberty and start using your age to project the confidence and common sense that go with it. Remember, the companies interviewing you have a definite need to be filled. Your task is to indicate to them just how your experience will satisfy that need.

Apologize for your age either in words or dress and you'll never get hired. Use it positively and you'll be amazed. And incidentally, you should know that job discrimination based on age is now against the law.

C. L. Mallon, V.P. for personnel and labor relations with Goldblatt Brothers, echoes a familiar theme. "Anybody over forty we love," he states cheerfully. "They have a better attitude. They come to work even if they don't feel well." He was referring, of course, to the horrendous absentee rate among younger workers.

On the other hand, if you are convinced you are too young for a given job, think again. *Nation's Business* reports: "Age has less bearing on searches for chief executives than it once had." Today hundreds of major companies are managed by men and women in their late twenties and early thirties. In some businesses, younger than normal managers are considered a fashionable sign of aggressiveness. "The young managers are more than willing to hop from company to company if a new job offers more money or promotion possibilities," reports *Time.* "That is one reason why older executives tend to view them with a predictably paternal mixture of unease and affection."

In an interview, take the trouble to encourage this "paternal affection." Listen to what they say. Actively seek their advice. Convince them that *your success depends on their help.* They will quickly perceive you as a partner, not a threat.

FIVE

Eleventh-Hour Tips

Take a refresher course

Take the oldest advice on record

Take notice of the little people. They can make
you or break you.

Take it easy

T HE night before *the* big game, athletic coaches tell their teams to go to a movie, read a good book, look at television . . . do anything that will take their minds off the coming challenge. Good advice for jocks, perhaps. Bad advice for you.

TAKE A REFRESHER COURSE

Long ago, students cramming the night before a hard exam discovered the incredible capability of the human brain to retain an awesome amount of information, if only for a very short time. You, too, should put this capability to work.

1. Review *all* the material you have read or prepared.
2. Note *late-breaking news* which will be on top of your interviewer's mind: mergers, sales results, new contracts, etc.
3. Check your memory for the names and titles of all *key officers.*
4. Know the company's *financial situation.* Be able to verbalize it.
5. Review the *questions* your interviewer will ask you (see Chapter 3).

6. Organize and select the key *questions you must ask* (see Chapter 9).
7. Review all people and events which led up to the inter-view: letters, various individuals, etc.

Once you have this material clearly arranged in your mind, you will be able to conduct your interview from the beginning to the end without fear, and overdependence on irrelevant pleasantries or vague generalities. At the time when most candidates are throwing up smoke screens to hide their ignorance or panic, you will be armed with facts, insights and confidence which can't help but impress your interviewer.

TAKE THE OLDEST ADVICE ON RECORD

Nothing you can possibly do will destroy an interview faster than showing up late. Barbara Walters advises: "The most efficient way to demonstrate that you're reli-able and self-disciplined is to be on time. It's a good idea to arrive about five minutes early, in fact."

TAKE NOTICE OF THE LITTLE PEOPLE. THEY CAN MAKE YOU OR BREAK YOU.

The receptionist is usually the first person you will meet in any company. Remember, she is a person, not a ma-chine or a piece of furniture. Treat her like a human being and you will gain a valuable ally. Treat her like a servant and she'll get even with you in her own way.

Talk with her. Learn her name. Take a personal interest in her life and she will automatically take an interest in yours. With her sympathy you will get through to a busy executive faster than normal. You will have an easier time setting up second interviews.

Receptionists' lives are plagued with boredom. The very nature of their job forces them to live vicariously. This means they hear more and see more than most people ever realize. Underneath their cool exterior they are just dying to tell the world how much they know. So don't let the receptionist down. Let her tell you things about the company and your interviewer. Let her demonstrate her knowledge by asking her questions you wouldn't dare ask your interviewer. "How many people have interviewed for this job?" "How long has the company been looking?" "Who makes the big decision?" "Why hasn't someone within the company been offered the position?"

The next person up the ladder can be absolutely crucial to the success of your interview: your interviewer's *secretary*. She is the person who schedules your appointments and reminds your potential new boss to return your call or answer your letter. She will type and sometimes even write your evaluation. How she feels about you, either positively or negatively, will certainly be communicated to your interviewer.

Therefore, learn her name. Whenever possible, enlist her help in your cause. Most secretaries have a very close working relationship with their boss. A good word from her may have more value than your best references. Whatever you do, don't take her for granted, ignore her or, even worse, insult her if your interviewer forgets an appointment with you or fails to return your call. Most bosses feel that "he who insults my secretary insults me."

TAKE IT EASY

Tomorrow you're going to have a good time. There is no reason to be nervous. Inteviewing can be great fun, especially when you have done your homework and have therefore virtually eliminated the element of surprise.

Pretend you are talking with a friend. This doesn't mean being overly familiar. It means being relaxed, not visibly tense. Avoid calling him "sir." Remember, many interviewers are more nervous than the people they are interviewing. Don't try to impress him right off. This will make him suspicious, and besides, your turn will quickly come. Help put *him* at ease. There is no need to launch straight into business. Let some small talk ease the way until you both are relaxed. The weather, artifacts on his desk, some local news event, some harmless piece of company gossip are always safe openers.

Easy does it with your vocabulary, too. Use words you are familiar with. Let your personality unfold naturally. And forget any foolishness you may have read about where to sit and what to do with your hands. Choose any chair that looks most comfortable if he does not point one out. If you want to smoke, ask his permission. Stay loose. Successful interviewing is an exciting game. The more you enjoy it and the more your enjoyment shows, the better it will go.

SIX

Your Attitude Will Get You Hired

There is no substitute for enthusiasm

Always tell the truth, sometimes

You're the best person he'll see all week

Get him to like you without being a sycophant

Don't knock old bosses

Don't be a snob

MORE people win interviews and get hired on the basis of their attitude than on their qualifications. Young job hunters find this difficult to believe, but few corporate chairmen would dispute it. Attitude is the ultimate measure, the final arbiter, of even the most difficult hiring decisions. And just as your qualifications can be developed, so can your attitude.

THERE IS NO SUBSTITUTE FOR ENTHUSIASM

If you don't have it, drop out of the game right now. If you can't or won't develop it, all you have is my pity. If you have to fake it, save yourself a lot of heartbreak and don't try. Samuel Goldwyn, the colorful, immensely successful producer of Metro-Goldwyn-Mayer fame, put it all rather simply: "No person who is enthusiastic about his work has anything to fear from life."

In life, nobody likes a downer. In business, they simply don't get hired. Addressing himself to people just beginning a business career, John Paul Getty ranked "enthusiasm" well ahead of business acumen, ambition and even imagination: "It is one of the most important of all qualifications a beginner can possess and it can compensate for many other shortcomings." PepsiCo's chairman Donald Kendall chimes in, "I favor young men and women executives who are enthusiastic, innovative, 'on fire' with the work they're doing and carrying the same attitudes into their families and communities."

Defining the "enthusiastic candidate," ITT's recently retired chairman Harold Geneen was characterized by *Business Week:* "Nothing matters to him but the job—not the clock, not your personal life, nothing." Barbara Walters capsulizes her own experience and that of countless corporate executives I have interviewed: "The main element in landing the job is, believe it or not, how badly you want it. Employers these days put a premium on enthusiasm and zeal because they are fed up with employees who regard their jobs as places to display their wardrobes while waiting for life to begin at five o'clock."

The fact that you communicate your enthusiasm in your interview is, of course, essential. How you choose to accomplish this is all-important. Perhaps it is helpful to define enthusiasm, from an employer's point of view. We are *not* discussing the Archie-comic-book, golly-gee-whiz, do-I-love-your-company type of enthusiasm. We are *not* talking about cheap flattery directed toward the interviewer, his product or the business in general. We are *not* talking about your personal enthusiasm over the possibility of finally landing a job and earning a paycheck, or your relief over getting off the unemployment line.

Enthusiasm, as seen from behind the interviewer's desk, looks quite different. When former General Electric senior vice president Hershner Cross says, "We look for people who have enthusiasm for their work," he is talking about a person who knows and loves his field. He is describing someone who avidly follows all the developments in his trade. Someone who holds interesting and strong opinions. He has in mind someone who enjoys discussing the most minute aspects of his business till the cows come home.

Fred Lazarus, Jr., the spectacularly successful former chairman of Federated Department Stores, describes the enthusiastic person as someone who probes below the surface: "You have got to be curious as to what makes the whole business tick and have the ambition and desire to fight to get to a place of more responsibility."

The board member and former chairman of General Motors, Thomas A. Murphy, interprets enthusiasm as a sense of higher purpose. "It's like the old story about the two men working in a quarry," Murphy explains. "The one is asked what he is doing and he replies that he is cutting stone, and the other is asked what he is doing and he says, 'Why, I'm building a cathedral.' That is the spirit you will find among GM people."

How you choose to project your enthusiasm in an interview is dictated by your personality and the type of interview being conducted. Like laughing, lovemaking, and crying . . . enthusiasm is a natural human emotion which can't be taught. Some people communicate this excitement without even using words: a twinkle in their eyes, an instinctive smile, an uninterrupted attention span, an impossible-to-describe electricity flowing through their bodies. Describing his boss, James V. Lester, president of ITT Europe, observed, "Geneen is great at observing facial reactions. He wants to see the interplay of the verbal as well as the written."

Some candidates bombard their interviewer with a series of totally spontaneous questions prompted by a sincere and profound interest in the subject. Many fearlessly
challenge the statements and opinions of their interviewer
when they find their own beliefs being contradicted,
questioned or mocked.

The grandfather of RCA, General David Sarnoff, said,
"Nobody can be successful in a organization if he doesn't
love his work, love his job." Biggies like Sarnoff instinctively look for this enthusiasm in the people they interview. When they find it they are gratified, appreciative
and, most important in any interview, forgiving. Through
a younger person's enthusiasm an older employer relives
his earlier days, reaffirming his own contributions and
purpose.

Conversely, the second he senses indifference, boredom
or opportunism he feels insulted and tricked. An unen-
thusiastic job applicant might as well be announcing that
his interviewer's life has been trivial and wasted. And in
his anger, the interviewer may lash out with unfair questions or cruel insights. And who can blame him? It is one
thing to have someone demean your life's work at a cock-
tail party; it is quite another matter to receive this treat-
ment at the hands of someone looking for a paycheck!

As I have already stated, genuine enthusiasm can be
encouraged, developed, but not learned. It must be instinctive. And yet, for some mysterious reason, many job
applicants feel that to express emotions like enthusiasm
is either unbusinesslike or simply out of place in an interview. Individuals who stifle this spirit are doing themselves a great disservice. The successful executive may be
cool and ruthlessly efficient to an outsider. But just below

this polished exterior surges a passion for his business that knows no bounds. Let him share his passion with you and your interview can't fail to be productive.

ALWAYS TELL THE TRUTH, SOMETIMES

"I don't know what made me blurt it out. The interview was going beautifully. I was seconds away from the job offer, when he said, 'Of course you've had statistical experience.' Naturally I said, 'Of course!'"

Instantly this innocent and anxious-to-please University of Missouri graduate initiated one of the most humiliating experiences of his adult life. A subsequent routine reference check not only uncovered his lie, but word quickly filtered to the two other companies he was interviewing.

Lying in an interview, on a résumé, in a letter, anywhere, is a foolish and serious mistake. Why? Liars eventually get caught, usually long before they snag the job they are after. *Personnel* magazine, reporting on a 1976 survey, reveals that "93 percent of the participating companies verify previous employment and 53 percent verify educational records." A more recent survey of various personnel and nonpersonnel interviewers reveals that verifications are being carried out with increasing frequency and thoroughness in all employment categories. The reason? Mushrooming incidents of lying, coupled with a tighter job market.

Checking an applicant's educational background is a time-consuming chore. New laws which protect a student's transcript from being released without his permission have created a paperwork nightmare that some lazy or rushed employers would rather avoid. Taking advantage of this situation, hundreds of thousands of job seekers regularly turn to their skills in creative writing when it comes time to fill in the "education" section of their résumé. No doubt the Harvard Business School has ten times the number of graduates their alumni records show. Current favorites among this year's applicants are the difficult-to-verify degrees from foreign universities like Heidelberg, Cambridge, the Sorbonne, and others.

Many employers have been stung so frequently over the last ten years that they are now reacting with a vengeance. *Personnel* magazine states that an increasing number of employees, often successful ones, are immediately dismissed when irregularities in their past records are discovered. Every year the *Wall Street Journal* prints stories of executives who are fired because of various untruths they submitted at the time of hiring. One General Motors executive was horrified to read his fabricated educational history printed word for word in a Detroit newspaper as part of his promotion announcement.

It is impossible to fault companies for demanding honesty. They have a perfect right to know what they are buying, just as you have a right to know what is entailed in the job they are offering. But what makes them apoplectic is not that someone managed to slip through the verification net onto the payroll. What frightens them to the bone is the knowledge that someone who lies once will probably lie again—even worse, that person may be unable to keep a secret. Companies doing classified defense work, companies facing desperate and hungry competitors, companies with serious internal personnel problems . . . these organizations simply don't need to carry the risk of employing untrustworthy people.

Of course, the biggest loser in all these situations is the applicant himself. So many careers have been scarred or ruined because an insecure job hunter wanted to award himself with an extra degree or a juicy piece of unearned experience. The real damage is often not inflicted by the company that discovers the lie, but rather by the word-of-mouth grapevine that can hound an applicant from interview to interview.

The business world is a small world. And negative news has a way of traveling faster and being remembered longer than most job seekers ever realize. Some unfortunate people have been branded for years or even drummed out of an entire field because of a particularly colorful or noteworthy untruth.

But the best reason not to lie is that it is not necessary. Everybody has aspects of their lives that are better left unmentioned in the interviewer's office. And you are certainly under no obligation to present your weak points side by side with your strong ones. Any salesman worth his salt knows this instinctively. If a particular dish soap doesn't clean quite as well as its competition, its advertising is perfectly entitled to ignore this fact and stress, instead, how good it is for your hands.

When you present yourself to an employer, when you are fielding tough questions, when you are put on the spot *. . . ignore the negative completely.* Present only the positives. This can be a tough trick to learn, but it works miracles. For example:

INTERVIEWER: Mr. Smith, did you take accounting in school?
APPLICANT: For the last two years I have been working side by side with MBA's, and as you'll notice on my résumé, I've been promoted twice.

Note that Smith avoided answering the question with a blunt "no" and instead offered the interviewer concrete proof of his success.

INTERVIEWER: Mr. Jones, as a policy we don't hire people without sales experience in automotive hardware.

APPLICANT: You're right. Hardware is a difficult sales area, and that's why I am especially grateful for the experience I gained working for a retail chain in college.

Here, Jones cleverly agreed with his interviewer's point of view, then proceeded to neatly insert the sales-related experience that he did have.

Did either Jones or Smith lie? Of course not. Did they answer the interviewer's question? Weeell, not exactly.

Interviewers today are accustomed to thinning the number of job applicants with a pattern of tough questions or requirements that only a handful of people could satisfy. Don't let this discourage you. Don't play into their hands by giving up and admitting you're not qualified. You are, most likely, perfectly qualified for the job they are offering. But you may have to work like hell to prove it.

YOU'RE THE BEST PERSON HE'LL SEE ALL WEEK

"The first thing I look for is a sense of personal worth," says J. Paul Sticht, chairman of R. J. Reynolds Industries. "It's a subjective quality and hard to define, but I generally know when I see it." What Sticht goes on to define is a job seeker who is confident of his own abilities and purpose, a man who is not afraid to be judged with, or compared to, his contemporaries.

Talking about his own experiences in this area, Aristotle Onassis announced, "I have no friends and no enemies—only competitors." A rather cold-blooded admission perhaps, but this single-minded sense of purpose will serve you well during the short time you spend being interviewed.

The business of getting hired is a ruthlessly competitive race. The starting gun goes off the second you enter the interviewer's office. You won't see them, but you are running with a pack of competitors—ten, fifteen, maybe twenty-five other candidates your interviewer has already seen, or will see shortly.

The big difference between you and the pack is that you have a lengthy head start. Because you have thoroughly investigated the company, the interviewer and the job being offered, you are way out in front. Fewer than 2 people in 100 are this prepared for an interview. Don't blow your lead.

"People who get ahead," observes Xerox president David Kearns, "are those who prove they can get things done." And you are best prepared, because through your homework you know what has to be done. You know how to explain your skills in terms of his problems, *as he perceives them.* While other applicants are rattling off their credentials helter-skelter, you are focusing your questions and answers directly on his immediate needs.

Successful men in successful companies are by nature worrywarts. They are obsessed with potential problems months or years in the future which may threaten their growth or existence. "A successful business is built on two basic premises," says John G. Martin, a director at Heublein, Inc. "One is ideas and another is people who can come up with ideas and soundly administrate and execute them." Once again, since you have studied the company, know its competition, you can demonstrate sympathy and understanding for these long-range concerns.

Once you express your familiarity with these concerns and fears you immediately have a leg up. Suddenly, in the middle of the interview, you can become an insider, gaining valuable trust. Because you know a company is secretly concerned about an expiring patent on a very profitable product, you can help define your role in the company when that eventuality comes to pass. Because you are familiar with some obscure proposed government legislation, you have automatically demonstrated that you may be in a position to help. Companies are always reticent to discuss their biggest fears in public. But in the privacy of an interview, they are more than willing to listen to any suggestions.

An interviewer's favorite defense mechanism is that "we really don't need anyone right now." Don't you believe it, even if you suspect that it may be true. Virtually all companies, except the smallest, can always use talented and aggressive new people. You simply must demonstrate *why they need you.*

Some executives find it easier to announce what they don't need. And this information can be helpful. Tom Watson, the brilliant founder of IBM, observed, "Business tends to grind people down. The difficulty of being creative becomes greater, and in his late thirties and early forties the average fellow is likely to say, 'I'll just keep my nose clean and stay in my niche.' Well, we have more of this than we need at IBM!"

Henry Ford II hints at the desperate need for thick-skinned team players who won't fly off the handle when one of their ideas gets thrown out the window. James E. Robison, founder of Indian Head Mills, wants people who are "optimistic and loyal," suggesting that perhaps he's had his share of job hoppers and gloom-and-doom executives.

A successful job hunter is essentially a salesman. He must aggressively sell his favorite product . . . himself. If he is too embarrassed or too lazy, he will fail. He must firmly believe that he is the best person his interviewer will see.

GET HIM TO LIKE YOU WITHOUT BEING A SYCOPHANT

There is some very dangerous advice floating around the interview circuit originated and perpetuated by people who probably have never had to go looking for a job. "Don't try to be liked," they preach. "Your ability to perform the job is all that matters."

Nothing could be further from the truth. It is a terrible chore to talk with someone you don't like, much less hire him. F. Carl Schumacher, Jr., president of Hickey-Mitchell Co., says. "It's human nature that most of us want to be liked by those around us. That goes for even the toughest executives." GM's wizard, former chairman Alfred Sloan, said "personality represented 75 percent of the necessary equipment" for executives he interviewed. Derich Daniels, the president of *Playboy*, remembers that in his own job interview with Hugh Hefner, "the meshing of personalities was all-important." When Scott Paper's former chairman Thomas B. McCabe was asked how he could spot a person with executive ability he answered,

"You are generally attracted by his personality and ability to deal with people."

Your interview is no different. If your interviewer likes you, he'll relax. If you like him, you'll relax. When this happens you are on the road toward winning the interview. First, he'll give you the benefit of the doubt on tough questions. Second, he'll start empathizing with you, remembering when he was in your seat a few years back. Third, he'll accept your attributes with ease and often without question.

Most executives, certainly those with responsibility for hiring, have their days filled with company politics and tough interpersonal clashes. For the few moments they spend interviewing you, they don't need more of the same. In most cases, they instinctively want to like you. So let your personality unfold. Don't be afraid to be human. Xerox's Peter McColough confesses that he's "attracted to the man or woman with a sense of humor, especially the self-deprecating kind."

What exactly affects the chemistry between two people in an interview is difficult to assess: maybe the weather, the events of the day, perhaps even the stars above play a role. A fascinating survey published in *Personnel* magazine reveals that "some employers like applicants most like themselves—in height, weight, cultural background and personality." Other executives look for qualities they don't have. They appreciate personality traits and qualifications which complement gaps in their own character or background. Early in your interview, you must establish which group your interviewer belongs to.

Large multinational companies look for people whose personalities are adaptable. Because these employees are constantly moving all over the globe, they need men and women who can be easily relocated without facing difficult readjustment problems. Mike Wright, former president of Exxon USA, says, "You weigh his ability and background for the job. His personality has something to do with it because he has to get along with people." Exxon has no fewer than 130,000 people to get along with!

Anyone who assumes that bootlicking is part of being liked is in for a big shock. An executive with any responsibility at all can smell a sycophant a mile off. He's surrounded by them eight hours a day. And that's not why he's interested in you. Harold Geneen has a lot of company when he says, "I don't want a man to 'yes' me to death."

The job seeker who has researched his interviewer will find himself in the best position to develop a strong, amicable relationship. If, for example, you know you'll be facing a real cold fish, you won't make a fool of yourself trying to warm him up. Instead, you'd be wiser to approach him on his own terms: efficiently, politely, with caution. On the other hand, if you are interviewing a colorful character who loves to tell company "war stories," you may wish to flatter him by suggesting some familiarity with his tales. But tread lightly. Heavy-handed flattery is just another form of bootlicking and can quickly finish your chances.

An increasingly important element in the delicate chemistry of interviewing involves letting the interviewer notice other aspects of your life. Sticht of R. J. Reynolds Industries, sounds a familiar theme: "I admire men and women with controlled energy. They are not just work-aholics but utilize their energies beyond their company—

in their family and community involvement, for instance."

PepsiCo's Donald Kendall echoes this sentiment. "Corporations are no longer islands unto themselves," Kendall observes. "And managers moving up must utilize their skills and experience to improve life about them." Reginald H. Jones, chairman of General Electric, agrees and adds that "managers of the future will be less provincial, more world-minded." Union Carbide's chairman William S. Sneath confesses that he places extraordinary weight on a person's involvement in his community's affairs.

Companies today are looking for, sometimes demanding, balanced individuals . . . what Geneen calls "good all-around guys." Job hunters who belong to school boards, other community groups and various reputable organizations have a definite interviewing advantage and shouldn't be nervous about using it. Xerox's McColough speaks for countless others when he says, "I believe that a person who lives what I call a balanced life is likely to be more effective in a corporation." In other words, all other things being equal, the candidate who belongs to the United Fund board, the volunteer fire department, the Junior Chamber of Commerce will probably get hired first.

DON'T KNOCK OLD BOSSES

The late, legendary General David Sarnoff, probably hired, fired and interviewed more medium- and high-level corporate executives than anyone else in recent history. In his career of building a massive electronics company, the incredibly successful NBC radio and television empire, not to mention publishing, recording and other related industries, Sarnoff had intimate contact with more than his share of geniuses and phonies. Like so many chief executive officers, he constantly found himself having to evaluate people whose areas of expertise he only vaguely understood. And yet, over the years, Sarnoff demonstrated an uncanny ability to pick good people.

No doubt Sarnoff depended heavily on internal advice from RCA management. But in the final analysis, he was his own man, making his own decisions. "The first and foremost ingredient of leadership is to have *confidence* in yourself," Sarnoff stated. "Because if you lack confidence in yourself you won't have confidence in other people either." Sarnoff's unique ability to spot that confidence in an interview became famous. And the one thing that revealed its absence most was an individual who laid his problems at someone else's feet.

The job applicant who turns on his current or former boss to elevate himself is really turning on himself. It is one of the most common and serious blunders job seekers make. It is a major reason why many perfectly qualified people don't get hired.

During your interview, simply make it a hard and fast rule: *Never be negative!* There are bad, weak and unfair leaders in every company. Your interviewer knows this better than you do. He knows that if you were totally satisfied with your present job, you wouldn't be in his office.

Besides, nobody likes a whiner. He doesn't really care if you got a raw deal at your present job. His interest is understandably selfish. He wants to know what kind of job you will do for him, at his company. And the second you start knocking your old boss he'll begin wondering, and rightly so, how long will it be before you start in on him?

All of us have an ego. And we'll go to great lengths to protect it. In your interviewer's case, protection may mean deciding not to hire you. Don't let this happen.

DON'T BE A SNOB

There are all kinds of snobs—social snobs, intellectual snobs, athletic snobs, corporate snobs. Snobs are bullies. They use a real or more often a totally imagined sense of superiority in one particular area to elevate themselves in all areas.

Social snobbism has suffered a serious setback in the last twenty years. But it is still alive and well in countless companies, large and small. As a job hunter there is virtually nothing you can do about this situation when you encounter it. But you can monitor your own behavior and save yourself a lot of trouble.

Don't let yourself start dropping the names of people or places that are not directly related to the job, your interviewer or his company. If he senses that you are trying to impress him in this way, he will loathe you. Talk about private clubs and special organizations are a definite no-no, even with the bluest of blue-blooded interviewers.

On the other hand, never apologize for who or what you are. For what it is worth, these days WASPs are "out." Ethnic is "in." Silver-spoon upbringing is a big negative. Somebody who has had to work for what he has is a much more attractive candidate. Barbara Walters says that every time she faces a difficult interview, she remembers some advice she received from Abigail McCarthy, "I am the way I am. I look the way I look. I am my age."

While social snobbism may be disappearing, corporate snobbism is quickly taking its place. And in many ways it is just as ugly and objectionable. Today people place a great significance on their corporate affiliation, to the eternal irritation of nonmembers. The kind of person who announced that he is a "Princeton man" in the forties is today telling us with the same arrogance that he's "with Bankers Trust."

Corporate loyalty is fine and dandy. But worn as a badge of superiority, it is quite objectionable. Your interviewer is, no doubt, quite familiar with the company you now work for. He has his own opinions, which may or may not be positive. One fact is certain. His loyalty is with *his* company. And you had better respect that.

SEVEN

Self-Defense in the Event of an Attack

Turn the stress interview into a piece of cake

Testing: The corporate paper tiger

Your sex life has nothing to do with anything

Gimmicks and cheap shots

VIRTUALLY all interviews of any real substance contain a section which *you* may characterize as a personal attack. In most cases this is not an attack at all. Sometimes the interviewer may be testing the depth of your beliefs in a particular subject. Sometimes you are actually being flattered either by the intensity of his interest or by a last-minute stress check before he offers you the job. Often the interviewer will be following a highly structured interviewing technique. Or perhaps your interviewer is simply bored and wants to spice up his day at your expense.

Whatever the situation, this part of the interview is not to be feared. It is really an opportunity. And because you are prepared, this is yet another chance to separate yourself from the pack—a chance to demonstrate that you are the person he should hire.

TURN THE STRESS INTERVIEW INTO A PIECE OF CAKE

The stress interview in its various forms is a devilish little technique of questioning designed to shake your confidence and send you floundering off into a series of contradictions and ego-damaging statements.

In all likelihood you have probably survived the stress interview in the past without even knowing it. It is nothing more than a structured approach to the old lemon-squeeze or the fraternity hazing session with a few CIA/KGB twists thrown in.

The classic stress interview, now widely discredited and rarely used, was developed by a former Nazi concentration camp prisoner named Kurt Einstein. "We don't care what a man's views are," explains Einstein, "We just want to know how his mind works." Einstein outlined a very aggressive questioning technique which employs flattery, sarcasm, disbelief and wild accusations.

In theory, the unsuspecting applicant, caught under a barrage of insults, untruths or totally irrelevant statements, begins to contradict himself or lie. And, presumably, the interviewer gains some special insight into the candidate: his erratic quirks, abnormalities, weak points, etc. A typical question might be: "Let's suppose you or your child must die tomorrow. If you die, the rest of your family will starve to death. If your child dies, the family has food. Which alternative would you pick?"

It is not hard to understand why this insulting interviewing technique quickly faded after a burst of momentary popularity in the early sixties. However, a handful of interviewers still use it. And if it is ever your misfortune to stumble onto one of these psychotics, I suggest you leave his office, write a letter of protest to his chief executive officer and eliminate that employer from any further consideration.

There are other relatives of the stress interview which are widely used and considered fair play by many professionals. Former President Jimmy Carter underwent a mild version of it when he was being interviewed by Admiral Hyman Rickover for a place in the nuclear-submarine program.

"He [Rickover] began to ask me a series of questions of increasing difficulty," Carter remembers. "He soon proved that I knew relatively little about the subject I had chosen. He always looked right into my eyes, and he never smiled. I was saturated with cold sweat. Finally, he asked me a question and I thought I could redeem myself. He said, 'How did you stand in your class at the Naval Academy?' I swelled my chest with pride and answered, 'Sir, I stood fifty-ninth, in a class of eight hundred and twenty!' I sat back to wait for the congratulations—which never came. Instead, the question: 'Did you do your best?' I started to say, 'Yes, sir,' but I remembered who this was, and recalled several of the many times at the Academy when I could have learned more about our allies, our enemies, weapons, strategy, and so forth. I was just human. I finally gulped and said, 'No, sir, I didn't always do my best.'

"He looked at me for a long time, and then turned his chair around to end the interview. He asked one final question, which I have never been able to forget—or to answer. He said, 'Why not?' I sat there for a while, shaken, and then slowly left the room."

The military and military-related businesses have always enjoyed using stress-type interviewing techniques, apparently with some "success." An underling of Robert McNamara, Secretary of Defense in the Kennedy Administration, remembers: "To be interviewed by McNamara is like being picked over by bees!" McNamara is widely credited with a comment now so popular among

professors around exam time: "You don't know the answer if you can't explain it."

Corporate interviewers across the country use stress
techniques regularly. "Some interviewers are deliberately
cold to determine whether your composure will stand up
to it," Barbara Walters observes. "Don't get angry and
don't get anxious," she cautions. "Just wait it out."

Quite often an interviewer will deliberately try to make
you lose your temper. When you feel yourself being
sucked into this trap, simply stop talking. Take several
deep breaths. Reply very calmly and politely. Be evasive,
if you must. What these interviewers are trying to establish is whether or not you have the emotional fortitude to
hold up under a stress-filled job. *The second you blow your
stack, you've lost the job offer.*

When you find yourself edging into panic or even
becoming mildly flustered, it is often helpful to turn the
conversation back toward your interviewer. Ask him to
redefine the question or to be more specific. Very often
the interviewer will skip the matter altogether and move
on to the next item on his list.

Occasionally, humor can be your savior. A smile, a
laugh or a question like "Is that a question you learned in
the CIA?" Let's face it, a large percentage of interviewing
is role playing. Many interviewers ask the same questions
and get the same answers for years on end. A refreshingly
honest and different reply can be not only endearing but
also very rewarding.

The stress interview can also be deceptively friendly.
"If the interviewer takes the pals-together approach,"
Barbara Walters warns, "don't be misled into telling her
or him *all.* One girl lost a job she wanted badly because

she felt cozy enough with her prospective boss to tell him that her hobby was witchcraft."

Too many job candidates, relieved by the friendly attitude of their interviewer, volunteer a lot of unnecessary and quite often damaging information. Don't ever be tricked into thinking the interviewer is your new best friend. He's busy taking notes on everything you say and in his own quiet way he is looking for reasons why you would not be a good employee.

Jimmy Hoffa, hardly an example for young or old job seekers, did offer one excellent piece of advice. On his desk he had a sign which read, *"Illegitimi non carborundum,"* or in plain English, "Don't let the bastards wear you down."

TESTING: THE CORPORATE PAPER TIGER

The comedian Ed Wynn claimed that he landed his first job many years ago simply on the basis of a single test administered by two personnel assistants. One looked into his right ear while the other peered into his left. He qualified, Wynn said, "because they could not see each other."

Shortly after World War II, colleges and graduate schools began cranking out graduates armed with degrees that related specifically to personnel management and hiring. Many large companies snapped up these highly trained professionals to man their personnel departments. Basically, these men and women brought with them a background in psychology and a blind faith that testing of one kind or another could accurately determine almost anything, including which job candidates would make successful employees.

Corporate management, thrilled that something so im-
partial and scientific could solve their difficult selection
problems, bought the idea hook, line and sinker. Middle
managers in any organization, government, schools or
companies are always anxious to escape responsibility for
sensitive decisions. With the advent of testing, suddenly
their career was not on the line if someone they just hired
decided to embezzle company funds. In addition, it was
simply a lot easier to administer a battery of sophisticated
tests than it was to conduct a thorough, in-depth interview.

In time, of course, senior corporate management discovered that the candidates with the best test scores did
not always make the best employees. And personnel people began a slow retreat, suggesting that the tests needed
refinement and that perhaps they were only part of the
selection process.

A 1976 survey of 200 corporate personnel directors
revealed that less than 42 percent were still administering
psychological tests. *Personnel* magazine reported: "Companies are putting significantly less emphasis on testing in
making hiring decisions. Instead, they are relying more
and more on screening interviews, employment interviews, application form data and references." Defensive
personnel people like Dr. Frank J. McCabe, a former psychologist with ITT, admitted, "We don't have any right
answers. There isn't an ITT profile."

Until very recently it seemed that testing, under attack
from all sides, including the powerful Office of Equal
Employment Opportunity, was doomed to oblivion. But
suddenly, in 1978, the *Wall Street Journal* reported a strong
resurgence among major employers like Delta Air Lines,

Sears, General Electric, Union Carbide, IBM and J. C. Penney.

"There is no major company that isn't at least experimenting with some form of psychological assessment," says Paul Sparks, a psychologist and co-ordinator of personnel research at Exxon Co., USA. But the battle is still being fought. "The whole idea of psychological testing is personally distasteful to me," asserts Lawrence Klamon of Fuqua Industries, an Atlanta-based diversified manufacturer. "Just how far can a company go before it starts trampling on the rights of its employees or potential employees? What next? Hiring private investigators to see whether a job applicant has any skeletons in his closet?"

It would be comforting to inform you that you will definitely not have to face any psychological testing. That is not possible. And if a company has testing requirements, you should cooperate, willingly. Understand, however, that the results of this *testing are almost always ignored in light of a successful person-to-person interview.*

The most widely used tests attempt to measure your skills, ability, intelligence and personality. These tests are often not significantly different from other tests you may have taken in school. In some cases, they may be the very same. Often employers use them simply to evaluate your writing ability, a subject which obsesses so many corporate leaders like Henry Ford II.

A small number of companies, less than 4 percent, are sufficiently concerned with employee honesty to require polygraph (lie detector) tests. This requirement, now highly controversial, is not, in my opinion, unreasonable in light of their special needs. Different from other test-

ing, polygraph testing is totally single-minded and is not
used to evaluate your personality or job-related abilities.

Finally, there is one kind of testing which not only is
growing in popularity each year, but which you should
eagerly anticipate—the pre-employment physical exam.
More than 75 percent of major companies today require
this quick doctor-conducted checkup before you start
work.

YOUR SEX LIFE HAS NOTHING TO DO WITH ANYTHING

A job interview is not the third degree. You are free to
pick up and walk out anytime you please. And there are
times when you should. But before that possibility pre-
sents itself, you should know the law and carefully evaluate just what your prospective employer has a right to
know and not know.

Most of us are familiar with court rulings about race
and religion. We know that employers cannot ask us
which group we belong to and that they may not advertise or otherwise preclude candidates on this basis. In
addition, there are innumerable other decisions designed
to protect the job hunter.

Of interest to women in particular, the following is a
partial list of information which may *not* be solicited by
an employer under penalty of law.

    Your age
    Your weight
    Your sex
    Your marital status
    Your engagement
    Your present living situation

Your children's ages
Your arrangements for taking care of them while you're at
  work
Your plans to have more children
Your relationship with your ex-husband or ex-wife

Of concern to men and women, the following is also against the law for employers to inquire about:

Your criminal record
Your military background (name of service, type of dis-
  charge)
Your living accommodations (Do you own or rent a home?)

Some of these rulings are qualified because of the unique character of a job in question. An employer looking for a men's-room attendant certainly has the authority to inquire about a candidate's sex. But if you are pressed on any of the matters above, you should know that you can contact your local Equal Employment Opportunity Office and be assured that your interviewer and his company will quickly find themselves in hot water.

The intent behind many recent court decisions is obviously to protect women who have been entering the job market in increasing numbers. Having long been victims of discrimination, women have needed and now largely receive effective legal protection.

However, all the laws in the world can't force an employer to hire you, except in very rare instances. Laws don't help you win interviews either. Just the opposite, in fact. For this reason you should make an effort to understand some items which concern employers, and take them into consideration.

A major concern among all companies interviewing

women is their commitment to the job. Bluntly, they want to know if you are planning to have more children. Their fear, often quite justified, is that they will spend large sums training you or place you in a particularly sensitive position only to have you leave for several months or perhaps forever. They are worried that your husband may be transferred out of town and that you will, naturally, follow him. If you're not married, they worry that you may soon marry a man who doesn't want his wife to work.

These are all legitimate employer concerns. And while it is strictly illegal for them to ask if you're taking birth-control pills or if you're in love with a man who's being transferred to Saudi Arabia, you can at least understand why they would want to know.

In many cases you may want to *volunteer* information which will strongly enhance your chances. If you're sure you don't want any more children, why not tell your interviewer? If you have reasons why you would never move away from the area, don't keep them a secret. If you have a reference or previous employer who can testify that you never missed a day's work despite the fact that you have thirteen children . . . get the news out.

In short, try to second-guess your interviewer's concerns, and whenever possible, reassure him that hiring you will not be a mistake. Robert Cassidy, human resource manager at Continental Corporation, recently suggested: "Because of the new laws in many states and because of potential new federal or state laws, you would be better served to disclose more about your background rather than relying on the interviewer to draw it out."

Many women, blacks, and other groups which historically have been victims of hiring discrimination are often put off by their newfound popularity among employers anxious to right old wrongs or gain favor with government. Juanita Kreps, former U.S. Secretary of Commerce and the first woman to hold this position, urges these people to use perspective. "I don't think you have to shy away from tokenism," Kreps says. "It's not such a bad thing. It's just a stage we have to go through."

"I have concentrated all my life on seeing that I never had to spend my life in the kitchen," says Mary Wells Lawrence, chairman of Wells, Rich, Greene, Inc., a massive New York advertising agency. "I'm not aware I'm even a woman until after five o'clock. If you're willing to really get out and just work your little head off, I don't care if you're green, purple, blue, female or male . . . you have a very good chance of accomplishing the kind of life and life style you want to accomplish."

GIMMICKS AND CHEAP SHOTS

The interviewer's office has always been fertile ground for a host of pseudopsychological tricks that are supposed to produce great insights into the character and qualifications of an applicant. In most cases, however, they reveal more about the interviewer's brain capacity than anything else.

Men and women who conduct large numbers of interviews invariably develop their own interviewing format which they apply universally to one and all. This format is usually laced with various questions, techniques and idiosyncrasies which they have developed and polished over the years. Many interviewers defend this standardized interviewing as a method of maintaining objectivity from one applicant to another. I have long been convinced that laziness is their real motive. Customizing each interview requires a lot of hard work—work that most employers, especially personnel people, are simply not up to.

One particularly tiresome personnel man at a large electronics corporation near Boston has begun each interview with the same flimsy gimmick for more than fifteen years. Feigning an air of great importance, he proceeds to address the applicant by the wrong name. How the applicant chooses to correct this intentional error supposedly provides revealing information on the candidate's self-image. This personnel man, pointing to a file with thousands of various responses, told me that this information is "priceless."

The number and variety of these gimmicks is impossible to guess. Yet a few of them have become favorites over the years and you should be on guard. The "wiggly chair" trick is a favorite among old-timers. By making one of the chair's legs shorter than the others, the interviewer can amuse himself as the applicant's nerves are rattled loose by a chair that lurches back and forth. Presumably, this asinine technique is designed to test your confidence. I suggest that if you find yourself wobbling in this manner, test your interviewer's confidence by suggesting that he have his chair repaired.

Each year thousands of job hunters who smoke are confronted with the classic booby trap—the missing ashtray. It is probably best to avoid this time-honored setup by pretending that you don't smoke. Many employers today, not to mention interviewers themselves, disapprove of smoking, anyway.

The light-in-your-face trick, popularized by gangster movies in the thirties, continues to crop up with regularity. You're not Edward G. Robinson and your interviewer isn't Elliot Ness, so politely ask him if he would mind moving the light, which is in your eyes.

A runaway favorite in the gimmick department is the "sell me this" test. Pointing to some knickknack on his desk, the interviewer may ask you to sell it to him under the pretext of testing your salesmanship and presentation ability. Most applicants jump into this situation with mock enthusiasm and quickly proceed to damage the interview by presenting an unstructured, repetitive and often illogical sales pitch. Don't let this happen to you.

You will be able to perform brilliantly if you have enough time to organize yourself. It is not necessary to sit in contemplative silence. Instead, begin to bombard your interviewer with key questions about his brass paperweight or whatever else he wants you to sell. While he is answering questions about how much it costs, who the potential buyer is, what useful function the item will perform, you will have bought enough time to pull your sales message together. Often his answers will give you strong selling ideas. Sometimes your intelligent questions will impress him more than your sales pitch.

If you are being interviewed for a sales position, the "sell me this" gimmick assumes greater significance. You must take this opportunity to demonstrate your knowledge of basic selling fundamentals. In many ways, what you say is not as important as how you say it.

Interruptions are at the root of many bad interviews. Just as you are getting into the meat of your interview the phone rings and the man across the desk launches into a fifteen-minute conversation. Or even worse, in the middle of one of your sentences the interviewer excuses himself and leaves the office for a while. By the time the two of you get back to the business at hand, the momentum is lost, the subject under discussion is forgotten or confused, and the entire interview is a disaster through no fault of your own.

Unintentional interruptions occur with interviewers who are terribly disorganized, seriously overworked, rude, or all of the above. Intentional interruptions, where the interviewer instructs his secretary not to answer his phone or where he invents an excuse to leave the office, are increasingly common.

But whatever the reason for the interruption, there is only one loser: you. And you must not let this destroy the precious few minutes you have with your interviewer. When you are interrupted, make a specific mental note of exactly where the conversation left off. It is *your job* to pick up the train of thought and reconstruct the conversation. Naturally, if you are lucky enough to have the interruption save you from a difficult question or a dangerous line of thought, let the interview proceed to the next topic.

Remember, this interview is your chance to present yourself in a positive light. You must make it successful. And you can't expect the employer to share your level of interest. Tomorrow he'll be talking with someone else. If interruptions have totally destroyed your possibilities, you must definitely ask him if you can reschedule another time. Don't be hesitant on this matter. Your interest in his company, your confidence in yourself and your perseverance are all attractive traits employers look for and appreciate.

A very powerful interview weapon is *silence.* It has a way of making unprepared job seekers practically wet their pants. Typically, an interviewer might ask a routine question like "How do you like your present job?" After your brief response, the employer might say nothing. Most candidates interpret this silence as a sign of suspicion or a nonverbalized request for additional unpleasant details. Don't fall into this trap. Don't clutch over a break in the conversation and begin motor-mouthing. You will only give him useless or even damaging information.

When you are faced with silence, look him in the eye and give him a dose of your own silence. He'll break the ice first. If not, ask him if there is anything else he would like to know. Silence is powerful stuff. Use it wisely.

Another popular cheap shot you will probably face is what interviewers call "forced choice" questions. For example, an interviewer might say to you, "Most of our executives enjoy playing golf. Do you?"

Many unprepared candidates will blurt out "yes" even if they hate the game with a passion. Immediately they have fallen into the trap of providing answers they think will please the interviewer. These answers often produce the opposite results. Answer all questions carefully—and most important, honestly.

The group interview, an interview between you and several members of the company all at once, is relatively common with certain employers and for certain jobs where team-oriented work is found. Don't let it throw you. Unprepared candidates often panic in anticipation of a gang attack, when in fact this type of interview is often the easiest of all.

In this situation you will find it very productive to ask

a lot of questions. Direct each question to a particular person, not to the group. In his effort to answer you, he will be very careful not to embarrass himself in front of his fellow employees. He will often assume a defensive and cautious position, putting you in firm control. If the session should take a nasty turn, keep the same principle in mind. Formulate the toughest questions you can and address them to the person you think would have the hardest time answering them. This simple technique will enhance your position, though regrettably, at the expense of an employee.

EIGHT

When to Shut Up

If he'll talk about himself, egg him on

Let the gossip get juicy

Keep your skeletons in the closet

The job may be a bummer

When you think you've been hired

Most of us talk too much. Especially when we are deep into our very favorite subject . . us. This tendency can be counterproductive in a job interview. Without exception, anytime you suspect that what you are saying isn't constructive, useful information your interviewer wants or needs to hear before he hires you, shut up. As a rule, try to listen twice as much as you talk.

IF HE'LL TALK ABOUT HIMSELF, EGG HIM ON

As a job-hunter, one of the luckiest things that can happen to you is to stumble upon an interviewer who either enjoys talking about himself or who can be coerced into the same. This relieves you of a difficult obligation and opens up a valuable source of information. It greatly enhances the development of positive interpersonal chemistry so important in winning interviews.

Every interviewer is a human being with an ego just as healthy as yours. While his job is to evaluate you, have no doubt that he finds himself infinitely more fascinating. The moment he lets that ego creep into the interview, you must embrace it with diplomatic passion.

The first step, of course, is to let him talk freely without interruption. Pay very close attention. Let him sense that you are seriously interested in his every word, even if what he is saying has little to do with you, the job in question or even the company. Avoid gushing with admiration. This can be quite transparent and your rapt attention will have the same effect.

As soon as you sense that the subject at hand may be exhausting itself, be prepared to jump in with questions that quickly reinforce the depth of your interest and prolong his monologue. If he is talking about his own career with the company, ask him how he got started. How did he become so successful? How many people report to him? Does he still love his work? Egg him on carefully, with the impression that you have never met anyone so successful in your life. Ask him questions which will help him empathize with you. What were his own interviewing experiences when he was looking for a job? Did he ever imagine way back when that he would ever be so successful?

Don't be afraid of being a stooge. Believe it or not, you are gathering priceless information which you will be able to use with devastating effectiveness later on in follow-up interviews, letters and phone calls.

Corporate chairmen and other successful senior officers have always recognized and appreciated the art of effective listening in the interview situation. Philip D. Armour, founder of the giant meat-packing firm, bluntly admitted, "Most of my success has been due to keeping my mouth shut."

Remember, every interview is a meeting of two salesmen. You, on one side of the desk, are trying to sell yourself. "I can tell any young man that if he follows the rules of successful salesmen, he won't talk too much," General Tire & Rubber's L. A. McQueen cautions. "He will let his prospect talk."

Your interviewer, on the other side of the desk, is selling his company. Your well-directed questions, patience and eagerness to listen will make his job easier. And you will benefit. "You've got to encourage the reluctant speaker," suggests Du Pont's powerful ex-chairman Crawford Greenewalt. "But the guy who wants to talk all the time," warns Greenewalt, "must be graciously shut up."

LET THE GOSSIP GET JUICY

No matter how much research you have done, you can never hope to keep abreast of company gossip. And, for the most part, this is fortunate. Because this information can get you into big trouble. And how!

Companies are like families. They thrive on plenty of infighting. But, let an outsider butt in or even imply something off color and suddenly they will close ranks and unite against him instantly. Leonard Goldenson, chairman and founder of ABC, once delivered a classic denial about a corporation which literally thrives on vicious gossip and politics. "We have a family spirit," Goldenson snarled to a reporter. "No politics, no intrigues."

However, certain gossip can be very useful in helping you make important decisions and evaluations. For instance, if you learn that your interviewer is out of favor, about to be fired or passed over . . . this is important. If you hear that it is next to impossible to get a decent raise

... this is *very* important. If you discover that the company may be tumbling into bankruptcy ... this is *vitally* important. Gossip which is interpreted wisely can help you in a thousand ways, including the most basic decision of all: whether to accept the job or not.

How you interpret the importance and validity of gossip is tricky business. If, in the course of your interview, you pick up gossip which concerns you, ask yourself what could be the purpose of this rumor? Is it only wishful thinking on the part of the person who is spreading it? Does it echo other gossip you have heard previously? As much as you can, try to piece together where the gossip originated and who the beneficiaries are.

It has been my experience that virtually all company gossip is based on at least some truth. But how this is interpreted by the person who delivers it to you can be wildly inaccurate. Therefore it is necessary to double- or triple-check an important rumor among people whose interests are at cross-purposes.

For example, if you hear that a company is in a dangerous fiscal position, try to carefully sound out this rumor among people on the financial side of the company as well as someone in sales or production. They may contradict each other, but their choice of words, their sense of concern, their general attitude will help you evaluate this crucial matter.

Several years ago employees and job candidates at Union Carbide Corporation began to hear rumors that their company would be moving out of New York City. Various line people speculated that they would be moving north into suburban Connecticut because the chairman wanted to live closer to the office. A financial officer implied that while a move was unlikely, New Jersey would receive prime consideration. Meanwhile, senior management responded by asking inquisitive reporters where they had heard this unusual rumor? The absence of a flat denial by senior management should have been the first definite clue that in fact the company would soon be relocating.

In every company the employees can be broken into two uneven groups: the "ins" and the "outs." The significance of every rumor should be measured according to which group is delivering it. The "ins" are the smaller clique, those currently in favor with company policymakers. When rumors begin breaking you can count on the "ins" to defend the company line to the hilt. If management wants to discourage or deny some rumored event, the "ins" perform their duty with faithful enthusiasm. Generally speaking, these people jealously guard their status in the company and go to great lengths to defend their relationships with their seniors.

The "outs" are slightly more paranoid. They often consider themselves victims of the "ins." Typically, they blame their failures on their unwillingness to act politically or on their sense of independence. By far the largest amount of gossip originates with the "outs." Much of it is either grossly exaggerated, sour grapes or wishful thinking. Some of it is disarmingly accurate.

As you sift through company gossip trying to ferret out the truth, consider carefully the motives of both the "ins" and the "outs." Make sure you know which group your interviewer belongs to. But, *never allow yourself to take sides, or even worse, pass along rumored information.* Zipper your lips and listen carefully.

KEEP YOUR SKELETONS IN THE CLOSET

During a friendly, informal job interview, many applicants become overconfident and begin to introduce damaging, unasked-for material. The second you feel this
temptation, STOP TALKING . . . in mid-sentence if you
must. You must never be negative in a job interview
. . . especially about yourself.

Unless you are specifically asked, there is no reason to
volunteer the fact that you were fired from a previous job
or that you've had a drinking problem in the past or that
you occasionally indulge yourself in transsexual fantasies.
If an employer is concerned about your health, credit
rating, family life or anything else . . . let him ask.

No one in this world has the slightest obligation to sell
against themselves. You will never hear a Pontiac salesman tell you that a Dodge will get better gas mileage. And
you will never win an interview if you assume that your
interviewer has the compassion or understanding of a
priest or headshrinker.

Besides the obvious negative details which can destroy
an interview, all job hunters should be careful when revealing personal tastes and desires which may pertain to
the job. An out-of-town applicant interviewing for a job
in Denver would be advised to minimize his enthusiasm
for skiing. Give an employer a chance and he will use an
applicant's snow fever to negotiate a lower salary. For
years San Francisco employers enjoyed special advantages
because so many job seekers were willing to sacrifice
money, benefits and increased responsibilities just for the
opportunity to live in the Bay Area.

THE JOB MAY BE A BUMMER

In their enthusiasm and anticipation over an expected job offer, too many applicants simply stop listening. When your interviewer begins to describe the job he has to offer, don't interrupt and listen very carefully. Neatly tucked into his patter may be some very good reasons why you might be happier working elsewhere.

Keep your ears cocked for a slip of the tongue that may give away a major negative. For instance, you may learn that the last 5 people who held this position quit the company. You may discover that the job entails 9 1/2 months of traveling a year. Or that you will be obligated to work on weekends, evenings, or to entertain out-of-town customers 5 nights a week.

Even more serious, you may learn that the company has no plans for promoting you, no matter how brilliantly you perform. Or that your basic personality may be in direct conflict with company policy.

Most company interviewers are well aware of whatever negative aspects the job entails. Rather than frighten you away by bluntly stating these potential problems, they often use euphemisms or obscure language when describing your specific responsibilities.

Tone of voice and choice of language will tell you a great deal. A good listener will be able to detect the difference between sincere enthusiasm versus mechanical, forced interest. If his description of the job lacks spark and spontaneity, an alarm should go off in your head. You may be the 44th candidate this week he has tried to bamboozle into signing on. He may have held the job himself and be perfectly aware of what a dead end it really is. He just may be doing you a huge favor by telling you in body language that you are too good for the job he has to offer.

Frequently, what the interviewer doesn't say about the job tells you more than what he does say. If you catch him stressing frivolous details, such as an extraordinary number of vacation days or extensive opportunities to enjoy golf with customers, you have a perfect right to suspect that the salary in question may be pitifully low. If he tries to impress you with the intimate contact you will have with senior management, you may be justified in suspecting that what he wants is a glorified messenger or "yes" man.

Continually be on guard against the "something-for-nothing" sell. When you begin hearing details or benefits that sound just too good to be true . . . watch out! There is sure to be a catch somewhere or the position would have been filled earlier. When he says "We need a man who enjoys trout fishing," he may be implying that they eventually want you to relocate to northern Alaska. When interviewers stress "creativity" they are quite often describing a job with a boredom factor second only to a toll taker on the thruway. A job that is "perfect for someone with imagination" may be a job that is hopelessly swamped in paperwork and approval levels. A job with "excellent advancement possibilities" is usually a position much lower than you were anticipating.

Every business and profession has its own code words, ripe with inner meanings. You must learn this language and be able to understand exactly what is being offered, or not being offered. When in doubt, take notes during your interview and explore the matter in greater depth after the interview is over. Never allow yourself to be seduced into accepting a bad job simply because you were too lazy to listen to what your interviewer was telling you.

WHEN YOU THINK YOU'VE BEEN HIRED

Most of the time you'll begin to feel it almost instinctively. Something he says. A tone of voice. An abrupt change in attitude. A sudden relaxation of tensions. If your senses are alert and your antenna is up, you will know when the time comes. And it is important that you do know. Because a surprise job offer can sometimes be disastrous.

Here are several universal signs that a job offer is on the way:

1. *When the interview has lasted longer than 30 minutes.* Most interviewers block out their time in half-hour segments and they don't like to keep other applicants waiting, cut into their own lunch hour or waste any more time than is necessary on applicants who are not going to be hired.
2. *When the interviewer begins to sell his company with increasing urgency.* You can be sure he wouldn't be wasting his breath on a loser. Sit back. Listen carefully.
3. *When he suggests that you meet other people in the company.* This is a sign that you have won his interview and are well along the road to a job offer.
4. *When he starts talking about a different position than the one you came to interview for.* This usually means you have succeeded so well that he is about to offer you a job with more responsibility and salary than you expected.
5. *When your interviewer reveals that he knows more about you than either you or your résumé have told him.* If he has gone to the

trouble to check out your background in greater depth and chooses to introduce this information into your meeting, don't interrupt him. Most of the time this is a form of thinking out loud, a ritualistic summarizing of your qualifications just prior to a job offer.

This delicate period immediately preceding a job offer is just the time when so many unprepared candidates destroy their hard-earned success. "I'm particularly pleased to see someone make a point in a simple, forceful manner," states Henry Ford II. "On the other side of the coin, I have an aversion to pretentiousness and long-windedness."

The classic mistake many inexperienced salesmen and job hunters make is to fail to recognize the point at which the sale has been made. Too often, they keep right on selling and end up selling themselves right down the drain.

In the interview situation, you are the salesman. When your senses tell you that you are succeeding, order that mouth of yours to clam up. Your interviewer needs nothing more from you than your flattering and undivided attention to his closing remarks. Don't let him or yourself down.

NINE

Some Key Questions You Must Ask

IRONICALLY, the single most neglected aspect of interviewing is that area which should concern you the most: "Is this really the job for me?" The job hunter who tells his interviewer he has no questions is making a classic error which often results in either losing the job offer altogether or becoming entrapped in a job he never wanted in the first place.

These questions you must ask will serve two vital purposes. First, they will enhance your candidacy. No interviewer can fail to be impressed by serious, probing, carefully thought-out questions. Good questions may indicate that you are ready for a position of much greater responsibility. They will help you gain a higher salary. They will help your interviewer remember and select *you* out of a sea of qualified applicants.

Secondly, these questions will help you through the difficult decision process. Should you take this job offer? Would you be better served to wait and have more interviews?

What follows are several basic questions which every candidate should cover. You will notice that many of the more obvious questions about the company have been

omitted. These are questions which you have already answered, because you are one of the very few who has
done your homework on your employer. In addition to
the list below, you will want to ask questions of your own
especially tailored to the specific company that interests
you.

1. *"Why do you want someone for this job?"*
Force your interviewer to explain why this job can't be
done by one of his current employees. This will give you
a valuable job description.

2. *"Why isn't this job being filled by someone within the company?"*
You may discover that nobody in his organization
would accept it, or that your future fellow employees are
a weak lot.

3. *"Can you draw me an organization chart so I can see just where
I fit in?"*
Here's the point where you discover just who your real
boss will be, how significant your responsibilities will be,
your rank in the lineup.

4. *"How many people held this job in the last five years?"*
If the turnover has been high, you have a right to suspect that the job may leave something to be desired. Or,
it could mean that you can expect to be promoted quickly.

5. *"May I interview the person(s) who had this job last?"*
If your interviewer is reluctant to let this happen, you
should be suspicious. If he cooperates, follow up on this
important interview.

6. "Was the person who held this position promoted?"

7. "What do you like most about your company? Least?"
Someone in the personnel department may give you a relatively worthless answer, but anyone else in the company is well worth listening to.

8. "What are your biggest problems?"
Listen carefully, you might be walking into a hopeless situation. Or, you may be just the person they need.

9. "How has this position been filled in the past?"
Internally?

10. "What are some examples of the best results produced by people in this job?"
Here you may discover you are overqualified or in a position to ask for considerably more money.

11. "How many people are you interviewing?"

12. "What do I have to do to be promoted?"
If this question makes your interviewer nervous or uneasy, it is reasonable to expect that he has little desire to promote. On the other hand, if he explains, be sure to take careful notes. This information could be useful before and after you are hired.

13. "What are the company's future plans and goals?"
Can you picture yourself happily employed 3 or 5 years from now? Is your interviewer exaggerating? Does his

projection conflict with what you have discovered in your homework?

14. "How does this company treat its employees?"
Pay close attention. Listen for inconsistencies. Do they offer valuable benefits you were not aware of?

15. "Who owns the company?"
This is an important question if the company is privately held. You can be certain that the individuals with controlling interest will play a vital role in your future.

16. "What qualifications are you looking for in the person you need?"

17. "What exactly would you like to have me accomplish in this position?"
Is your interviewer being realistic or is he describing an 18-hour-a-day job that will lead you straight into divorce court?

18. "Can you afford me?"
Dangerous question, but quite effective if your interviewer is really desperate.

19. "How many people do I supervise?"
Obviously, this is not a question for recent graduates.

20. "How do you feel about their (people who report to me) performance?"
Be careful you are not walking into a hornet's nest.

21. "How does their pay compare with what they could receive elsewhere?"

22. "What is the biggest single problem facing your company right now?"

Your interviewer's answer may give you an important opportunity to offer valuable suggestions, further enhancing your candidacy.

23. "Will you be asking me to relocate out of town?"

24. "How soon will you decide if you want to hire me?"

This question can save you a lot of anxiety and also gently nudge your interviewer into making a quicker decision.

25. "Do you have any questions about my qualifications?"

Here's your chance to clear up any misunderstandings and come to terms with any reservations your interviewer may have.

TEN

Okay, So You've Been Fired. Here's Your Chance to Get a Better Job.

What not to do when the ax falls

Find out exactly what happened.
The real why.

Now put the truth to work

Watch your language

Trot out your references

BEING fired is not a sin, a crime or an embarrassment. It is an opportunity—an important lesson that too few people ever get to experience. It can be your chance to escape from a dead-end position or an unsuitable career. It can be a chance to earn more money and discover just how many companies, companies you never dreamed of, need your help immediately.

"If you want to be successful," says David P. Reynolds, chairman of Reynolds Metals, "you must also be able to profit from failure. Knowing how to handle the bumps is an outstanding trait of successful men. If you have never had a bump, a temporary failure or setback, then you have not set your goal high enough."

Getting canned can be, and should be, a whole new beginning. It can force you to consider a new career infinitely more satisfying and rewarding. Ask anybody who has been through the experience and he will tell you what most psychologists and counselors already know: being retained in a job you hate is more cruel than being fired outright.

Alfred C. Fuller, the man who perfected door-to-door selling, cherished the experience. "I was fired from my first three jobs," Fuller brags, "which in a funny way gave me the courage to go into business for myself." DeWitt Wallace used a similar occasion to found a modest publication called *Reader's Digest.*

WHAT NOT TO DO WHEN THE AX FALLS

Do not panic. Do not reach for the telephone. The biggest single mistake you can make is to immediately start spreading the word, sending out résumés and looking for a new job. If you have a job offer waiting . . . do not accept, no matter how tempting or comforting it may be. Do not explode in anger. Do not plunge into a sea of self-pity.

This is a crucial moment. A moment in which you can do yourself irreparable harm. You are the momentary victim of powerful anxiety, and perhaps guilt and anger too. You are in no condition to make rational decisions in your own best interests.

Stop. Freeze in your tracks. And *listen.* Listen to what is being said to you. Listen to what your own emotions are telling you. You are about to learn something that will help you find the best job you've ever held. You are about to turn a painful experience into an attribute, not a liability.

FIND OUT EXACTLY WHAT HAPPENED. THE REAL WHY.

Generally speaking, there are two reasons for dismissal: events within your control, and events beyond your control. The former would include action you took or failed to take which produced negative results within the company. The latter would include events you were powerless to prevent: a company merger or demise, the departure of your immediate boss, a change in company direction, a decline in profits. You must establish a clear understanding of which category your dismissal falls into.

You must understand the sequence of events and *real reasons* leading up to the dismissal—not what you wish they were, not what your friends may tell you they are, but the actual facts. And this is often no easy job.

Typically and understandably, a person stops listening the second he understands he is being fired. The explanation for dismissal falls on deaf ears as the victim is suddenly overwhelmed by the prospect of financial doom, social embarrassment or the nagging doubt that he will never regain his position/salary. You must find out, demand to know, the precise reason you were let go. This information is an essential ingredient in the formula you will soon need to find a better job.

Many companies offer written explanations, realizing that only after days or even weeks have passed will the dismissed employee be prepared to listen to and accept the truth. Most employers, however, deliver the word orally, and this can be a problem.

If you have any doubts, go back to the individuals responsible and calmly press for the truth, no matter how painful this may be. Some employers find the act of firing so unpleasant that they are unwilling or unable to tell you the truth. You must help them, explaining that it is imperative that you learn from the experience.

NOW PUT THE TRUTH TO WORK

What if your interviewer asks if you were fired? Admit it. Admit it freely. Applicants who hide the fact almost always get caught.

But don't bow your head in shame. Don't feel or behave like a failure. Never apologize. Virtually all interviewers agree that not only does complete candor on this subject help to exonerate you, it often makes you a more interesting candidate. Recently *Newsweek* reported: "Personnel experts say there's less stigma attached to being fired today than ever before." Jack Sidebotham, senior vice president of a large New York advertising agency, concurs: "Someone who has been seasoned under fire has learned an important lesson. They often have valuable experience that would be impossible to duplicate even with the most expensive training programs."

The moment the subject of your dismissal comes up, be prepared to offer your interviewer a short, well-organized and candid description of the events which led up to the dismissal.

Robert L. Swain, of Eaton-Swain Associates, a prestigious outplacement firm specializing in assisting discharged executives, puts the problem succinctly. "There are no virgins left," he says, referring to the large percentage of executives who have been fired at least once. "Contrary to popular belief, the major problem facing discharged people is not skittish employers . . . rather it's a matter of how a discharged job hunter feels about himself. If he refuses to acknowledge why he was fired, if he insists on carrying his blame and guilt into the interview, he rarely succeeds in finding the job he deserves. For this precise reason we advise that the individual spend a considerable amount of time preparing a *truthful,* forceful, positive answer to that dreaded question, 'Why were you fired?'"

Swain urges that the job seeker think of himself as a *product.* This attitude helps maintain objectivity and the volunteering of negative information. He reminds his clients that employers are interested in buying experience, not wounded egos. They want to know what you can do for them, not what you did wrong for someone else or how someone else did you wrong.

WATCH YOUR LANGUAGE

Words like "fired," "sacked," "canned" and "booted" are angry words pregnant with guilt, blame and resentment —sentiments that may sound threatening to your future employer and do you a disservice. You would be well advised to choose more descriptive words and expressions when referring to your dismissal. "My position was reorganized"; My job was eliminated"; "I had a policy disagreement with my boss"; "We agreed to part company."

As the interviewer presses for additional information, stress what you have learned from your past experiences and how this knowledge will directly benefit him and his company. Avoid expressions of bitterness and resentment. "Speak when you are angry," Henry Ward Beecher cautioned, "and you'll make the best speech you'll ever regret."

TROT OUT YOUR REFERENCES

Nothing can be more helpful in explaining a dismissal to a nervous employer than strong references. If you haven't already done so, obtain written references from key individuals in your last company. This quick demonstration of confidence will effectively terminate a negative discussion and move your interview onto more positive points.

And if there is any guilt on the part of your previous employer, use this to your fullest advantage. Suggest tactfully specific points you would like these references to cover.

Job seekers who have been dismissed more than once obviously have a more difficult problem. But strangely enough, it is not always the fact that you were fired that upsets employers. It's that long list of companies on your résumé that bothers them. A recent National Personnel Associates survey reports: "Too many jobs is still the number-one reason why applicants are turned down."

If you have had several jobs in a short period of time, you must be prepared with a clear explanation for your interviewer. You must put to rest his concern that his company will just be another addition to that list. You must give him carefully thought out reasons why this job will be yours for a long, long time.

One word of caution. While a previous dismissal is not a disaster, it is also not something to brag about. And just as you would never volunteer the fact that you were once a drug addict or a convicted felon, don't introduce your dismissal until asked. In an interview you must only volunteer information that is overwhelmingly positive. In short, don't answer the unasked question.

ELEVEN

How to Handle the 5 Gut Issues

"What's your GPA (grade point average)?"

"Why didn't you go to graduate school?"

"What are you looking for?" (Nobody ever says "money")

"What if your company gives you a counteroffer?"

"How soon can you start?"

A word about rejection

IN every interview there is at least one pivotal issue upon which the hiring decision rests especially heavy. Your ability to identify this issue early in the interview coupled with some preinterview preparation can make the difference between being hired or rejected.

Naturally, it is the interviewer's prerogative to choose the particular issue which he feels is the most important. What follows are several key issues which, over the years, have consistently concerned interviewers in all kinds of businesses from coast to coast.

"WHAT'S YOUR GPA (GRADE POINT AVERAGE)?"

Here is a question which should concern only young job applicants. And only those whose academic performance was mediocre or bad.

Many employers, it is true, are still perfectly willing to overlook a poor performance in school. "I look for common sense before intellectual brilliance in a leader," says Xerox's Peter McColough. "Yes, I do believe in late starters. I think that some bloom earlier than others."

"I have known many efficient, even brilliant executives," said John Paul Getty, "who received only mediocre marks in school." Talking about himself, Howard Johnson reveals: "I think one of the things that helped me a lot was the fact that I knew I wasn't a college man. So I had to try twice as hard as the other guy did." ITT's former chairman, Harold Geneen says, "All we are asking for is balanced men of average, or moderately better than average, intelligence with a willingness to learn and work."

However, recent surveys among major employers indicate that after a brief hiatus in the sixties, student grades are once again becoming a major concern, especially with those corporations who operate popular training programs. If your performance in school was weak, you must face this situation directly and be prepared to come to terms with it.

Yes, it is still possible to win your interview despite poor grades. But to do this you must effectively replace your scholastic record with something of greater importance. That "something" should be tangible evidence of your ability to work extraordinarily hard and perform well.

Every employer understands and appreciates the student who has worked his way through school. If you held a money-earning job in school, do not fail to introduce the fact at the earliest opportunity. Outline the job in specific terms. Make a point of indicating the number of hours of work each week. Volunteer to your interviewer the amount of money earned and how this money was spent. Make certain he has a clear idea of the time pressures you were under. Give a reference from your job and strongly suggest that he contact that reference.

If your job in school involved training or skills which would complement the job you are being considered for, skills like selling, managing, accounting, etc., point this out. Make a concerted effort to position this valuable experience as an important part of your overall academic experience.

On the other hand, if Daddy paid your school bills while you had a good time, don't try to hide the fact. Most employers will know when you are lying and can easily check out your story with one quick phone call to the college records office.

Instead, you should take a hard look at your scholastic performance and attempt to present yourself in the best possible light.

Many courses, as you know, are graded on a "pass/fail" system. Don't hesitate to point this out if it applies to you. If you are interviewing during the spring or early summer, it is fair to announce that you haven't received your grades yet. Many large schools are notoriously slow sending out final grades.

Some young job seekers find it advantageous to announce their ranking in the class rather than use a cold numerical grade. There is no question that ranking in the "upper third" of your class sounds better than a "2.9 GPA."

Rather than revealing your entire 4-year average, you may be better served volunteering just your senior-year average or the average for your last semester or trimester. Know which figure is best and answer the question accordingly.

As I have stated before, under recent legislation, *schools may not release your grade transcript to an employer without your written permission.* Employers, of course, know this. And if they ask for your cooperation you must comply if you wish to be seriously considered. However, many applicants find that if they enthusiastically volunteer this permission early in the interview they may succeed in blunting a difficult issue. Their confidence and openness will convince some employers that there is no real need to actually see the transcript.

"WHY DIDN'T YOU GO TO GRADUATE SCHOOL?"

Without a doubt the best one-liner reply to this question is, "Because I couldn't afford it." But this doesn't always let you off the hook. There is much more at stake in this question than most applicants understand.

Employers ask about graduate training because they feel it is important, if not necessary, for the job. And you must convince them that you have other qualifications and experience which more than make up for the absence of an advanced degree.

Perhaps you took graduate courses while still in college. If so, point this out. Perhaps your undergraduate training was focused on graduate subjects. Your interviewer should know this.

If you have had previous employment experience which may have given you graduate-type training, outline this experience so that your interviewer can convince his superiors that you are indeed qualified.

If you are planning to attend graduate school in the evening and earn your degree while also working, your interviewer would be interested in hearing about it. Be prepared to give him full details so that he will take you seriously. Tell him the school you will attend, the courses you will take and when you expect to earn that degree.

Many applicants find that it is helpful to pepper their conversation with graduate school lingo. Often this convinces nervous employers that you will be comfortable and hold your own in a training program dominated by graduate students.

"WHAT ARE YOU LOOKING FOR?" (NOBODY EVER SAYS "MONEY")

Everybody has a difficult time discussing money. Most highly paid executives perpetuate this problem with their heartfelt though sometimes sanctimonious pronouncements. Harold Geneen, whose annual income from ITT exceeded $1 million, could afford to say, "You work for money to begin with, but not for long. After that you work for pride." Joyce C. Hall (Hallmark Cards) feels that "A good man will work much harder for reasons other than money. Some men work only for money, but they aren't really top-flight men. They don't get much fun out of life." Aristotle Onassis observed, "After you reach a certain point, money becomes unimportant. What matters is success."

Revlon's bombastic former chairman, Charles Revson, was one of the very few to ever publicly admit that "the best man is the bought man." Du Pont's Crawford Greenewalt confided, "I am worried about our future executives. What cleaner incentive could there be than money?"

Most job hunters in most businesses should approach the salary issue with extreme caution. On one hand, they must not appear over-motivated by the almighty green-back. This is considered *bad business etiquette.* On the other hand, they must move carefully less they sell themselves too cheaply or overprice their skills for a job they desperately want.

If it is possible, and it usually is, postpone the money discussion until the last possible moment. This lead time will let you pick up salary hints from your interviewer, as well as give you an opportunity to do some last-minute homework before your second or third interview. If your interviewer begins to press you on salary requirements before you are ready, stall by asking more questions like, "Before we get to that, I'd like to know . . ."

You might find it useful to ask blind questions which ease you into position. For example, if you are *not* a recent graduate you might ask, "Just out of curiosity, what are June graduates getting this year?" If you have an MBA, you might ask what non-MBA people are starting at. Knowing this figure will help you estimate what you are worth.

At the moment of truth, your interviewer will probably name a figure. Judging from your experience during the interview and your knowledge of the company from your homework, you should know instinctively whether you can effectively counter with a higher figure you feel more comfortable with.

If your interviewer insists that you name your own figure, march ahead without flinching and *never look back.* Your chances of succeeding are excellent. If, however, you admit a willingness to negotiate, be prepared for him to take quick and full advantage of your weakness.

It was instructive to note in a current survey conducted

by Availabilities, Inc., that "unrealistic salary requirements" were not among the top reasons why qualified
individuals failed to get hired. Considering this fact, be
especially careful not to underprice yourself.

As a word of warning, that same survey noted, "Occasionally an employee has the attitude that he is the savior
of the industry and any employer should easily recognize
that and compensate accordingly." It goes without saying
that this kind of arrogance will produce only negative
results.

"WHAT IF YOUR COMPANY GIVES YOU A COUNTEROFFER?"

This question must not come as a surprise. You must have
an answer. If you don't, the nagging doubt in the interviewer's mind will destroy your interview.

If you decide to play the leverage game, pitting one
employer against the other, you are obviously undertaking a major risk. In most situations, you should never
reveal to a prospective new employer what you are up to.
If he senses that you are simply using him to leverage
yourself into a higher salary bracket with your present
employer, he will resent the fact and remember the situation for years to come.

The other half of the risk comes when you approach
your present boss with your new job offer. Even if he
decides to match the competitor's salary you may find
that you have destroyed an excellent working relationship and effectively torpedoed your future in the company.

If you are playing it straight, and generally it is best that
you do, give your interviewer an unequivocal "no" as an

answer. Put him at rest and improve your interview relationship with something like, "I've thought about that, but I don't believe in leverage interviews. The reasons I've decided to leave XYZ Company go beyond what the company can give me at this time."

"HOW SOON CAN YOU START?"

If you receive a job offer in your initial interview, and you very well might, *do not accept or reject the offer.* You have come too far, worked too hard not to give yourself the final advantage of some clear evaluative thinking away from the emotionally charged interview atmosphere.

Smile. Thank your interviewer. Then tell him that you need some time to consider his offer. He will understand and respect your request. If he reacts differently, you may be sure that his company is not the place for you.

Ask him for more time than you think you will need. The extra days you ask for can be used to negotiate with an employer anxious for you to start as soon as possible.

The time lapse between a job offer and final acceptance has another potential advantage which applicants should not forget. It is not at all uncommon for hungry employers to call back candidates they particularly like and "sweeten the pot" with a higher salary or increased job responsibilities. They do this, of course, to influence your decision. And you should welcome their efforts.

A WORD ABOUT REJECTION

How are you going to react when an employer decides not to hire you? Disappointed, of course. But *never angry.* This is too small a world to alienate an important and useful contact over your wounded pride.

True, you may have been rejected because your interviewer found someone he considers to be a better candidate. But, as so often happens, an employer may have suddenly decided that he couldn't afford you or couldn't use you at this particular time.

Perhaps there is one person you met during your interview who is blocking your acceptance. A cool, polite and unemotional posture on your part may be just the thing that keeps your name under consideration when the company lands a new contract or when the person who found you unacceptable retires, gets fired or moves to another position.

The moment your interviewer reveals his negative decision, you should immediately maneuver him into the position of helping you develop your prospective employer list. Ask him for names and advice. Use this brief period of sensitivity and vulnerability to your best advantage.

He very well may know the name of a company that would hire you today at a higher salary than you ever dreamed.

At the same time, again without being defensive, ask him where you fell down during the interview. Force him to elaborate in the frankest possible terms, no matter how much it hurts. Insist he be honest. Be willing to accept crucial information that will make your next interview a roaring success.

TWELVE

After You Leave His Office

Evaluate the interview

Fire off your letters

He won't forget you if you don't forget him. Call!

"THE only place success comes before work is in the dictionary," PepsiCo's chairman Donald Kendall reminds young job seekers. "The first qualification for success, in my view, is a strong work ethic." Rarely is this ethic put to the test more severely than during the 24 hours immediately following your interview. Like students who have just completed their last final exam, most job hunters think the pressure is off the second they leave the interviewer's office. Not true. This critical period requires every bit of energy and creativity you can muster.

EVALUATE THE INTERVIEW

From your interviewer's office go directly to a quiet place where you can sit down alone, pull your thoughts together and make some very objective notes on exactly what happened during the previous half hour. It is vitally important that you do this *immediately,* while your memory is hot and you can recall all key details. Nothing is more fickle than the human memory.

In diary style, write up an evaluation of what went on during the interview. Note *everything* that was discussed. And be specific. Include as many quotes (yours and his) as you can possibly remember. Be ruthless. Include all negative as well as positive points, regardless of whether you think they are important. Accurately record your impression of the interview. As objectively as you can, write down your interviewer's impression of you.

After this evaluation is completed, make two short lists on a separate sheet. On one list pretend that you are the interviewer and itemize in order of importance everything that your interviewer learned about you which he may have found especially appealing: your previous experience, education, appearance, attitude, whatever. Include only items that made you attractive as someone to hire, not as someone to like or enjoy talking with.

Start another list, again in order of importance, which includes all items which you feel may have damaged the interview or at least not have enhanced your chances of being hired.

Now put this valuable document safely away, get yourself a drink, go out for the evening, do anything you want which will take your mind off the whole subject until the following morning. You've thought about your career much too long and intensively to be productive at this point.

FIRE OFF YOUR LETTERS

Post-interview letters are an absolutely essential piece of job-hunting etiquette, regardless of how successful or disappointing your interview may have been. Applicants who are too lazy to make this simple effort are doing themselves irreparable damage, either for the immediate job at hand or for future benefits which they are too short-sighted to see.

On the surface these letters are "thank you" notes, expressing your appreciation for the time and attention you received. But their real function is much more serious —to enhance your candidacy. Whom should you write to? Write to every person you met during your interview who you think will have any effect on the hiring decision.

Each letter must be a carefully composed selling message. The ideal letter must do the following:

1. *Thank your interviewer for the time and attention which he gave you.*
2. *Reiterate your most positive attributes.* In one or two carefully composed paragraphs, outline those qualifications which you know he values and appreciates. This recapitulation will quickly remind him of who you are and why you should be considered seriously. Check your evaluation sheet before beginning.
3. *Counter negative impressions which may have been damaging.* As you attempt to answer these negatives, do not be negative yourself. Don't be defensive either. Using your post-interview evaluation list, choose no more than three negatives which you are sure you can counter effectively. "Although it is true that I have no international marketing experience, I have taken several graduate courses which indicate my aptitude in this area." Do not reintroduce negatives which you feel he may have ignored or which you can't overcome with several terse sentences.
4. *Introduce positive news.* The reader should learn some positive job-related information which was not revealed during the interview: special attributes, attitudes, training, experience, insights, etc.

Each letter should be *custom-tailored* for the person who will receive it. Often these letters are routed to several people and nothing is quite so insulting to receive as a form letter. Referring back to your evaluation sheet, mention points of common interest. "I have been thinking about your remarks regarding sales incentives and I . . ." Whenever possible, it is helpful to include clippings on important points discussed. You may want to mention some relevant piece of current company or business news.

Your letter should be in the mail no later than twenty-four hours after the interview, while your name and face are still fresh in his memory. Before posting, check the following points:

1. Do you have his correct name and title?
2. Is your language fresh? Does it communicate your personality and enthusiasm?
3. Is your spelling flawless? Is the letter neatly typed?
4. Will the reader take your candidacy more seriously after having read your letter?

HE WON'T FORGET YOU IF YOU DON'T FORGET HIM. CALL!

"If you persevere, and push and hang on long enough," Henry Kaiser advised both young and old job seekers, "you will wear down the opposition." Henry Ford II agrees. "I'm impressed by perseverance, understanding, consideration, openness and practical boldness."

If your interviewer said he would call you in four days but fails to do so, *you must call him.* If he was less specific, give him one week maximum, then call.

It is quite common for applicants to get pinned down in no man's land, and it is up to you to take the initiative. Sometimes key executives are on vacation or out of town on business. Often senior executives become reluctant to allocate the money for your salary. Occasionally executives with the final word on hiring become paralyzed in the decision-making process. Your telephone call can be useful in forcing their hand.

Be polite. But be tenacious. Remind your interviewer of who you are and very briefly summarize the positive points of your interview. Don't hesitate to remind him of any promises he may have made. Volunteer to come back to meet more people in the company. Offer to send in additional references or information which may be helpful. Often competitive job offers can speed the decision process, though this must be used with supreme tact. Nobody likes being strong-armed.

THIRTEEN

You're Hired!

When in doubt, trust your gut

How to say "no"

How to accept

You can win—one on one

As sweet as these words sound, they can cause more anxiety than you would possibly believe. For the applicant who is the least bit unsure about advancement opportunities, salary level and specific responsibilities, a sudden job offer can be quite unsettling. For the person waiting to hear from another company, or a counteroffer from a current employer, this news can cause unbridled panic.

In the interest of your career, let me repeat some important advice. The ultimate decision to accept or reject a job offer must be made by you and you alone. Never make this decision in the interviewer's office. Accept advice from friends and acquaintances, but the decision must be *yours.* Give yourself time to think. Time to maneuver. Time to develop firm opinions unfettered by a tidal wave of suggestions.

Once again, take out the written evaluation which you prepared immediately after your interview. Carefully weigh *all* the information. Use this sheet to make sure that you are not accepting a job which offers you less responsibility than you'll be happy with. It is terribly easy, and quite common, for applicants to begin assuming things which were never promised.

Are the negative elements which concern you real? They may be only superficial aspects which have little bearing on your career development. On the other hand, they may be insurmountable. How many marriages have gone on the rocks because one person thinks he will be able to change some dreadful character flaw in the other? A company with a strict policy of never letting salespeople grow into management positions is not likely to change despite your perseverance. A company that routinely sends its personnel to distant regional offices for two or three years of training is not likely to make an exception just for you.

All positive elements should be re-examined with the same ruthless objectivity. Just because a company is large, with a prestigious reputation in its field, does not mean that you are being offered a better job. A company that attracts you with additional vacation time or special bonuses may be blinding you to some serious negatives. An inordinately high starting salary may be tempting now, but what will you be receiving two, three or five years from now?

WHEN IN DOUBT, TRUST YOUR GUT

In many ways this is the most honest part of your body. Several job offers can look equal on paper, right down to the last detail. But your gut knows the right one for you.

If this gut-instinct decision-making makes you uncomfortable, take a moment and reflect on one important fact. The employer who wants to hire you was probably faced with an equally difficult decision, a decision which will reflect directly on *his* career. And in the majority of cases, this choice was not based on your résumé, your appearance or even your performance in previous jobs. His decision was a gut decision based on dozens of different factors, some of which it would be impossible for him to ever verbalize.

HOW TO SAY "NO"

Every day thousands of job seekers butcher this simple task. In a matter of seconds they destroy a precious relationship which could have served them for the rest of their working lives.

The man who has offered you a job is a priceless ally you can never afford to lose. To say "no thanks" and walk away is sheer stupidity. This interviewer may be hired as your boss at another company. Even worse, you may find yourself back in his office within a year begging for the job you rudely turned down. Sometime in the future you may need his advice or wish to call on him as a reference. The chances of both your careers affecting each other in the future is likely if not inevitable.

The most effective way to say "no" is to build a polite empathy between the two of you. Take the time to explain in detail why you cannot accept. Put him in your shoes. Tell him frankly how difficult your decision was. If the decision was especially agonizing, admit your concern that you may be making a mistake. If he becomes angry or curt, and he very well might, make an extraordinary effort to "keep the door open." Be honest and open during this difficult discussion and you will never regret it.

HOW TO ACCEPT

Don't be afraid to express your genuine enthusiasm, an emotion which probably played a key role in his decision to hire you. Pin down all the details, including salary, starting dates, insurance transfer, special bonuses, stock offerings, etc. To avoid confusion, it is often wise to ask for a letter of confirmation. This simple document outlines the important aspects of the job you have just accepted and eliminates the possibility of future misunderstandings.

Finally, once you have won the interview and accepted the job, *never renege*! Stand by your decision steadfastly. Failure to do so will give you a black eye that will haunt you for the rest of your career.

YOU CAN WIN—ONE ON ONE

All employers, in all areas of business, government and education, make their hiring decisions on the basis of a crucial thirty-minute one-on-one meeting known as the job interview. You can win this decision because you know what must be done.

Because you now know how to set up the right kind of interview with *the* person who controls the hiring decision, you can immediately eliminate much of your competition.

Because you now know how to prepare for your interview you are infinitely better equipped than the majority of the applicants your interviewer will ever see.

Because you now know how to ask and answer tough questions, how to maximize your strong points, how to defend yourself, how to dress, how to conduct yourself in all kinds of situations, you can walk out of any interviewer's office with the job you want and deserve.

ABOUT THE AUTHOR

A former advertising executive, THEODORE T. PETTUS now works as a consultant and free-lance writer. He has also worked on numerous presidential, senatorial and congressional campaigns.

Born in St. Louis, the author lives in New York City with his wife and two children.